DISAPPEARANCES

Also by Derrick Murdoch

THE AGATHA CHRISTIE MYSTERY

Derrick Murdoch

DISAPPEARANCES
True Accounts of Canadians
Who Have Vanished

1983
Doubleday Canada Limited, Toronto, Ontario
Doubleday & Company, Inc., Garden City, New York

Canadian Cataloguing in Publication Data

Murdoch, Derrick.
  Disappearances: true accounts of Canadians who
have vanished.

ISBN 0-385-17711-9

1. Missing persons—Canada—Case studies. I. Title.
HV6762.C2M87   363.2'336   C83-098056-3

Library of Congress Cataloging in Publication Data

Murdoch, Derrick.
  Disappearances: true accounts of Canadians who have
vanished

  1. Missing persons—Canada—Case studies. 2. Victims
of crimes—Canada—Case studies. I. Title.
HV6762.C2M87   1983   364.1'5
ISBN 0-385-17711-9
Library of Congress Catalog Card Number 82-45302

Contents

Acknowledgments

In preparing and writing this book I received helpful co-operation and suggestions from many sources. I particularly want to thank:

Eric H. Silk, Q.C., Commissioner of Ontario Provincial Police, 1963–73; R. A. Ferguson, Deputy Commissioner, OPP; Staff-Superintendent G. H. R. Cooper, Criminal Investigation Branch, OPP; Superintendent William Perrin, OPP; Inspector Atholl Smith, OPP; Inspector Carl Manneke, OPP.

Harold Adamson, Chief of Police, Metro Toronto (retired); Staff Inspector James Crawford and Detective Sergeant Vaughan O'Toole, both of Metro Toronto Homicide Squad; Sergeant Ernest Pollock, Commission Staff, Metro Toronto Police; Sergeant Joe Robson, Missing Persons, Metro Toronto Police (retired).

Sergeant Robert Udahl, Royal Canadian Mounted Police, Ladysmith, B.C.

Richard J. Roche, Chief of Police; Inspector Stan Waterman; Lieutenant Miller; all of the Royal Newfoundland Constabulary.*

Dr. Selwyn M. Smith, M.D., Psychiatrist-in-Chief, Royal Ottawa Hospital.

Hartley Nathan, Q.C.; Harry Cravit, Q.C.; Cliff Goldfarb; Joel P. Freedman; all Toronto lawyers.

Birnie E. Floyd, Civic Security and Investigative Services, Toronto.

Jack Evans, Executive Officer, Forensic Pathology Branch, Ministry of the Ontario Solicitor General.

Richard J. Doyle, Peter Moon, Ed O'Dacre, Jack Kapica, Richard J. Needham, Malcolm Gray; all of *The Globe and Mail,* Toronto; Val Sears and Jocko Thomas, both of the Toronto *Star;* Barbara Amiel of the Toronto *Sun;* Michael Harrison of the *Evening Telegram,* Newfoundland; Ted Byfield of *Alberta Report.*

Rosemary Lahey, now of United Church Family and Community Services, and Cissie Brown, both of St. John's, and Helen Porter of Mount Pearl, Newfoundland; Ted Ferguson of Edmonton, Alberta; Donna Henderson of Canapress Photo Service, my agent, Lucinda Vardey, my editor, Dean Cooke, of Doubleday Canada Limited, Sarah Murdoch and Carole Sacripanti, all of Toronto.

The Writers' Development Trust, Toronto.

The Ontario Arts Council.

Derrick Murdoch

* As stated in *Today's Back Pages,* the Royal Newfoundland Constabulary's activities did not extend outside the city of St. John's in 1979. This is no longer so. The Constabulary began policing a wider area around the city in 1982, and by 1983 will be covering most of the Avalon Peninsula. Plans call for its responsibilities to be expanded to areas of Labrador in the following year.

D.M.

DISAPPEARANCES

Whereabouts Unknown

To the family of the victim, any disappearance in any country can be a dreadful experience whether it lasts for only a matter of hours, months or years. Or forever. (Although the world being what it is, sometimes it's a matter of indifference or relief, even at the time it happens.)

To an uninvolved observer at a distance, the circumstance and nature of these disappearances tell a revealing story about the times in which they occur, prevailing standards of behavior, the state of the local economy and the degree of civil liberty.

Organizations like Amnesty International and many individual writers have given deserved prominence to the crimes of political "disappearance" committed under totalitarian governments. Other harrowing accounts have been written about young people who have disappeared while visiting Central or South America, and about the frightening compound of arrogance, inefficiency and official silence facing parents and friends seeking answers.

Those personal sufferings are very real, and it is right that they should be known. This book is not intended to supplement them. Its different aim is to show that in a fairly prosperous, civilized and peaceably disposed country like Canada, whose police, by and large, are decent, forbearing

men and women, disappearances, often inexplicable, also
occur daily. And that some of those disappearances are part
of the price to be paid for living in a relatively free democ-
racy. (If we were being continuously watched by secret police,
we would be safer from harm. Except, of course, from the secret police. Not an altogether attractive trade-off.)

Persuasive as this thought may be to that uninvolved observer it makes those disappearances no less emotionally
devastating to the families and friends sustaining the anxiety
and anguish that may follow.

Not all disappearances fall into that category. The individuals, or whole families, who vanish overnight to evade
their creditors and continue to elude the debt collectors; the
fathers in flight from child-maintenance orders; husbands and
wives who have found other loves: strictly speaking, none of
these count. If their whereabouts remains unknown for long,
it's generally because it would serve no practical purpose to
find them. I did not take them into account when I wrote
earlier that disappearances occur daily in Canada.

How many? It's impossible to be sure. As we'll see, some
disappearances are never reported to the police, and some, involving no apparent breach of the law or likely danger to the
individual, are not handled by the police. Beyond that, Statistics Canada apparently found that irreconcilable variations
existed in the ways in which missing-person information was
recorded in different police jurisdictions, making the figures
unsatisfactory for statistical comparison. Their publication
was consequently discontinued after the figures for the year
1977 had appeared.

Nevertheless, the collective figures are probably correct
enough to provide some idea of the size of the phenomenon.
They will probably surprise you. (Bear in mind that they exclude the categories which do not concern the police. They
also exclude children who were only temporarily lost at occasions like fairs, exhibitions and public meetings.)

On that narrowed basis, police officers across Canada accepted missing-person reports on a total of 25,731 adults and

62,587 young people and children in 1977. Assuming that the figures are at least substantially correct and that the situation has grown neither better nor worse, this suggests that more than 240 people, of whom about 170 will be young people and children, will be reported as missing sometime today in Canada.

Under the circumstances it is somewhat reassuring to find that the corresponding annual total of "Persons missing— Located" shows that the police were able to discover what had happened to 24,477 of those missing 25,731 adults, and to 61,338 of the 62,587 juveniles. In other words, they achieved an overall recovery rate of 97.2 percent—95.1 percent for the adults and 98 percent for the juveniles. Obviously, that took a lot of work, and meant that most fears were soon allayed.

But perhaps the figure is rather less assuring than it seems. The ambiguous word "located" does not necessarily mean that the missing persons were found alive and well. Some of those statistics have to stand for casualties and some for corpses. It cannot be overlooked that a total of 2,503 people—1,254 adults and 1,249 juveniles—remained unaccounted for at the year end.

In terms of daily figures, this indicates that of the 240 or so people who may be assumed to be reported missing sometime today across Canada, most will be found alive and unharmed. Some will be injured, a few may be found dead. But it seems there will be six or seven of them—three or four adults, three or four younger people—who will remain lost for a longer time. Possibly forever.

Here again, the figures can be deceptive. The fact that a missing person has not been "located" does not indicate that the police have no idea of his or her whereabouts; only that the indvidual, or the individual's body, has not been found and identified. Often enough these disappearances have taken place in circumstances or in locations that leave little room for unofficial doubt about what has happened.

In cases where missing people were known to have intended going into or near deep waters, swamps or remote

areas difficult to search, the probability of death by drowning
or exposure is clear. But unless sufficient tangible evidence is
available to establish the fact, the "missing" report must
remain open long after hopes for the individual's safety have
faded. They may also have to be reopened even after death
has been presumed, as two stories in this book tell ("The Man
Who Could Not Help Himself" and "Curiouser and
Curiouser!").

Similarly, unless a runaway requires medical attention
under medicare, or becomes involved in street activities at-
tracting the attention of the police, perhaps in a distant city, a
teenager's disappearance can often remain unsolved for a long
time. There is a limit to which the public feels the police are
expected to go in checking the identity of unknown teenagers
behaving in an orderly manner—as well as the time which
could be found to do so. But until the runaway is found, the
possibility of abduction, violence or even murder cannot be
disregarded, and the file stays open.

Nevertheless, there are probably only a handful of reported disappearances at any one time mysterious enough
and potentially ominous enough to cause good policemen to
worry long into the night. Even apart from errant spouses and
delinquent debtors, and apart from the unknown thousands of
illegal immigrants who have succeeded in disappearing into
the patchwork pattern of big-city life, there are, as noted
earlier, many other disappearances that may never be reported.

There are, for example, the unloved and unloving pre-
teenage and juvenile-teenage runaways discussed in the chapter "Runaways, Ramblers and Rascals," whose absences and
final disappearances are often more of a relief than a matter
of concern. There are the drifters, the small-time hoods and
informers of the underworld, unsettled and unpredictable,
whose disappearance may be a matter of temperament or of
prudence; often enough it is neither, but the consequence of
vengeance. Unless the body is found, perhaps in a deserted
building or the trunk of a stolen car or a lake or a sandy

grave, the disappearance may never become the subject of official investigation because nobody has reported it.

In respectable, law-abiding, middle-class life, too, the possibility of a disappearance remaining unreported, or at least unrecorded, seems to exist, as "Continental SuperFreeze Model 507" indicates. In that case the lengthy delay before the disappearance was officially noted appears to have resulted from the unlucky combination of a family in only occasional contact and a duty officer possessing more regard for "the book" than instinct for danger. There may have been others where the family could not bring itself to admit the possibility of disaster.

The chapters that follow cover a number of disappearances that have occurred in different parts of Canada over the past thirty years, as well as several recorded elsewhere and at other times, and cited here where comparisons may be useful. Some of these cases attracted national attention, others went barely noticed. Some had tragic or horrifying sequels, others remain unsolved. Many of those involving small children, youths and young women were so sadly similar and bleakly negative that a separate chapter was not required for each: grouped together as they are, they form a composite in which a pattern is discernible ("The Nestlings").

Certain forms of disappearance—the straying child, the adventurous traveler, the fugitive from justice, creditors or domesticity, the concealed corpse, for instance—seem to be constants at all times. The basic impulse remains unchanged, and although means of communication and methods of detection may have improved, the avenues needing to be investigated have multiplied at an equal rate.

On the other hand, different forms of disappearance seem to rise and fall in response to contemporary social conditions and pressures. In the brief period under review in this book, the newly emancipated but luckless middle-class teenagers like Mabel Crumback and Marion McDowell ("Yesterday's Headlines . . .") could be symbolic of the conventional 1950s, the swarms of juvenile runaways a sign of the rebellious 1960s, and the young children kidnapped by an estranged parent a by-product of the affluent but troubled 1970s.

Inevitably, crime and violence have a part in all but a few of the disappearances discussed in this book; sometimes horrifying, sometimes beyond normal comprehension, but occasionally in circumstances in which it might fairly be thought that the victim almost seemed to invite danger. In *Murder and Its Motives*, English author and criminologist the late F. Tennyson Jesse wrote that "there appears to be a race of human beings who lay themselves out to be murdered—they are murderees."

Some years ago there had been a spate of disappearances in England in which men had sought to conceal their murder of women who had become unwelcome in their lives by locking their bodies inside trunks which were, many months later, found to have been deposited under false names at busy railway left-luggage offices, leading F. Tennyson Jesse to recall:

> I remember once when talking to my hairdresser I said, more to make conversation than anything else: "And what do you think of this latest trunk murder, Mr. M.? Do you think they'll catch the man who did it?"
> Mr. M. replied, "I think so, madam, and I hope so." He paused a moment and then added thoughtfully, "But I daresay she was no better than she should have been. What I always say is: *You'll never find a nice girl in a trunk.*"

A preposterous as well as a prejudicial observation, of course, but somehow one senses the truth that the hairdresser proclaimed: some people ask for it. (And as far as trunk murders went, it turned out he was right.)

Some of the victims in the following chapters seem to me to fall within this classification, but I have tried not to indicate too clearly which I think those are. Opinions may differ.

Where the facts seem sufficient to allow a tentative conclusion to be drawn, I have indicated my own. But this is an open field in which all readers of detective fiction are welcome to join.

In a few instances, names have been withheld; in others, fictitious names have been used for non-central characters; this is primarily intended to serve as a study of an interesting and recurrent human phenomenon rather than as a reference source. Otherwise, however, all the factual information has been taken from the records or drawn from personal information and interviews.

What is here is the raw material from which fiction—dramatic, mystifying and often poignant—waits to be created.

All a Green Willow
Is My Garland

All a green willow, willow,
All a green willow is my garland.

The Green Willow,
John Heywood, 1497?–1580?

On Friday, September 17, 1976, Jack and Zetta Leeson collected Jack's sister, Viola Leahy, from the one-hundred-acre farm in Douro Township outside Lakefield, Ontario, to drive her, as they did most weekends, the short distance to Peterborough. There she would stay until Monday with the friendly woman she had met as a fellow out-patient at a mental health clinic in that city.

Viola, who was sixty-five and childless, got along famously with her forty-five-year-old friend. Soon, she could be sure, they would be sitting and chatting, or perhaps dancing, at the Queen's Hotel, or maybe the Trent Inn, with the two men of around their own ages who made up their social foursome.

These weekends, she often said, were what she lived for nowadays. Though she was always a non-drinker, conversation, laughter and music made her spirit soar. That Friday night, indeed, her gaiety at the Trent Inn apparently attracted the notice of a young stranger who drew her impetuously onto the dance floor and quite embarrassed her with the ardor of his advances, causing her to scuttle back to her table in giggling confusion.

Saturday also found them at the Trent Inn. On Sunday the foursome sometimes went to the movies, but this Sunday they sat and gossiped in Viola's friend's apartment. These were the times Viola could escape from her unhappiness and worries.

Before her marriage some twenty-five years ago as well as for some years following, she had worked as a registered nursing aide at an industrial plant in Peterborough; she knew enough to connect some of her worries to the diagnosis of arteriosclerosis her doctor had made some time earlier. She was still physically active, but a decreasing supply of blood to her heart could account for those memory lapses that were becoming more frequent. Unattended pots and pans burned dry. She hesitated to venture afield alone for fear she would forget the purpose of her journey. Lists had to be made of even the most routine task she had to undertake, and if she forgot to cross each item off as soon as it was done, she would be doing it again a minute later.

Probably it was the sense of insecurity this created that was responsible for her constant craving for company and entertainment. Unfortunately, her husband James, six years her junior, was unable to offer much of either. He spent long hours farming the lands four generations of Leahys before him had labored to cultivate, and had added substantially to those lands by undertaking heavy equipment work for neighboring farmers. When his day's work was finally done, he wanted little more than a beer, a meal, perhaps another beer, and an early night's sleep.

With temperaments so widely divided, discord had been inevitable. Four years previously, in fact, Viola had moved out, and since the property was jointly registered, an evaluation had been made as a preliminary to a legal separation. For some reason, however, they had attempted another, perhaps even bleaker, solution. Husband and wife occupied separate rooms, personal items like sheets and towels were kept apart, and each managed his or her own funds independently of the other. Viola undertook weekday cooking, cleaning and laundry in return for her weekend freedom.

In 1975 James had been badly injured in a farm accident. Nevertheless, although this greatly impaired his sight and required him to spend four months in Toronto's Sunnybrook Hospital undergoing extensive cranial surgery, the same cold relationship was resumed on his return. While he was in hospital, his brother Emmett Leahy and one or more of Emmett's sons had worked daily to keep the farm going. The Emmett Leahy family lived in a house purchased from James on an adjoining property to the south; normally, the menfolk only helped James out at harvest time.

When James returned, greatly incapacitated, Ralph Leahy, the second of Emmett's four sons, had continued to do some of the farm chores. But it was on her brother Jack and her sister-in-law Zetta that Viola had to lean for sympathy and support during the week. Jack provided most of her outside transportation, and she had dropped into the habit of phoning Zetta several times a day to maintain touch with reality during the week.

Perhaps it was the realization of how long it would be until the next weekend that made Viola phone her doctor in Peterborough from her friend's apartment on Monday morning, after her friend had left for work. She told him she was feeling unwell, and arranged to see him at six that evening on her way home.

Somehow she managed to spend the rest of the day by herself, and was ready and packed when Jack and Zetta arrived in the late afternoon. Their first stop was at her doctor's office; he gave her some pills, and advised rest. The consultation could not have been lengthy; they reached the farm at some time between six-thirty and seven.

Jack and Zetta saw her inside, and deposited her hand luggage in the front room before departing. At some time before seven-thirty, Viola called her friend in Peterborough, as she always did, to report her safe arrival, her appreciation of the weekend's social pleasures and her impatience for the coming of their next weekend.

And that, for nearly a year, was the last verifiable trace of her existence.

By midday on Tuesday, Zetta was surprised to realize that her sister-in-law had not phoned, particularly since Viola had said she was feeling unwell, and proposed spending the day resting at home. Finding Viola's phone unanswered through the rest of the day, Zetta told her husband they must go round the next morning to investigate. Jack agreed.

On arrival, they found the front door unlocked, Viola's luggage just where they had left it on Monday evening, and in the kitchen they saw an overturned flowerpot, and a couch pulled from its usual position against the wall. Knowing that neither Viola nor Jim smoked, they puzzled over the cigarette butts in an ashtray.

Finding no sign of Jim either, they decided they should see whether his brother Emmett could explain the mystery. Emmett said he certainly knew Jim's whereabouts; he had told Emmett that he would be returning to Sunnybrook Hospital on the previous Sunday, while Viola was in Peterborough, for removal of some bone fragments resulting from his previous surgery. But Jim had deliberately refrained from telling Viola in case she took advantage of his absence to fill the house with her friends. Emmett had no idea where Viola could be.

The next day he helped the Leesons to search the whole house, but they did not find any note or other explanation for Viola's disappearance. However, when Emmett related the search to his family that evening, his son Ralph said he thought he recalled seeing his aunt walking down the lane early on Tuesday morning in the direction of the bus stop.

When he told the Leesons of this, they hardly knew what to make of it. Viola so seldom went anywhere alone now or, for that matter, did anything of even minor importance without telling Zetta. Why had she left her suitcase unopened, and why was the furniture disarranged? Admittedly, her behavior was unpredictable, and finding how Jim had tricked her, she might have made an impulsive decision to retaliate. But where would she go? As they had already learned, Viola's Peterborough friend had not heard from her.

After another day without news, Jack Leeson accordingly reported his sister as a missing person to the Ontario Provincial Police in Peterborough on Saturday, September 25.

From the official point of view, some circumspection seemed advisable. Since the family was concerned about the lady's whereabouts, the circumstances had to be investigated. But the party concerned was not a child or even a contented member of a closely knit household. Viola Leahy appeared to be a discontented adult with some means of her own, who had a skittish nature and had left her husband once before. There is no law to prevent skittish ladies taking their leave, alone or accompanied, and it was reported that she had been seen on her way to catch a bus.

All in all, it did not seem a case for widespread publicity and alarm without grounds for suspicion that were strong enough to outweigh the danger of causing unwarranted embarrassment. No such evidence developed from the series of routine interviews that followed; everything appeared to support the view that Mrs. Leahy had simply responded angrily when she realized her husband had failed to tell her she would be returning to an empty house. Inquiries in Toronto, of course, had provided confirmation that James Leahy had indeed entered Sunnybrook Hospital on the previous Sunday—that is to say, while Viola Leahy was with her friends in Peterborough—and that it was expected that he would be ready for discharge in a few days.

James left the hospital, in fact, on September 30, but did not return to the farm until three days later, after visiting relatives in Barrie. When interviewed, he professed himself to be neither alarmed nor surprised by his wife's absence: she had done it before, he said, and since she had left so much clothing behind, she would doubtless be heard from soon enough.

But since there continued to be no information of any kind, the police decided to ask the Peterborough radio stations, CKPT and CHEX, to broadcast an appeal for information about the missing woman on Thursday, October 21. Among the several responses, there seemed to be two solid leads.

One was a call from a woman, a former nurse, who knew Viola quite well, and recalled speaking to her at the Queen's Hotel in Peterborough on a Friday or Saturday night some time in October, at least twelve days after her disappearance. Mrs. Leahy was with a man with whom she appeared to be on friendly terms the witness said; she was sorry she could not place the precise date, but she definitely remembered an Irish singing group being featured as the entertainment that night. And, sure enough, inquiries showed that the group had appeared at that hotel during the week ending October 9. Moreover, the description of Mrs. Leahy's male companion fitted that of her regular dancing partner well enough to support the opinion that she was on the loose and enjoying herself.

The second lead suggested where she might next be seen. By lucky chance, the broadcast appeal had been heard by the Lakefield postmaster, and he had recalled that only two or three days earlier he had received a change-of-address card requesting that all mail for Mrs. Leahy of R.R. ✕4, Lakefield should be forwarded to general delivery at a Sudbury post office—two hundred and fifty miles to the north. The card, signed in the name of Viola Leahy, had been mailed in Peterborough. The postmaster in Sudbury was promptly made aware of the circumstances, and asked to notify the police immediately if Mrs. Leahy presented herself.

But her redirected mail continued to accumulate, unclaimed. Among the envelopes were the Old Age Security checks she had become eligible to receive in the previous

July, and her Canada Pension Plan checks. Moreover, no
withdrawals had been made from her bank account, which
held a quite comfortable balance from her various investments. Even more disquieting in the increasingly bitter
weather, her furs remained in storage.

It was now evident that the disappearance of Viola Leahy
was not likely to have been voluntary. In the first week of
1977, the OPP division in Peterborough assigned one officer,
Provincial Constable Gary Katz, to work full time on the investigation. It had not previously been his case, but he had
from the outset doubted the runaway-wife theory. His feelings were strengthened when Viola Leahy's lawyer declared
that the signature on the change-of-address card received by
the Lakefield postmaster did not resemble his client's own
writing.

The fact that the card had been mailed in Peterborough
suggested that its sender lived locally. Katz had not yet met
all the people in Lakefield and Peterborough whose names
had come up in the routine interviews already conducted, but
he now set about collecting handwriting specimens to see
whether expert inspection could provide positive identification of the writing on the card. At best, this looked uncertain
since all the wording except the signature was in crude capi-
tals. In any case, the forgery so greatly increased the probability of concealed homicide that the Peterborough OPP recognized the desirability of calling in specialized assistance
from the Criminal Investigation Branch of the OPP's Special
Services Division in Toronto—Ontario's equivalent of Scotland Yard.

Detective Inspector Atholl Smith of the CIB, a senior
officer with close to twenty years of service, consequently arrived in Peterborough at the beginning of February. Taking
nothing for granted, he reexamined all the information already gathered. One early discovery was that the evidence
that Viola Leahy had been seen with a male companion at the
Queen's Hotel in Peterborough in the second week of October

was unreliable; the Irish singing group had also been performing at the same hotel in September.

Smith noticed something else, this time more positive. On the change-of-address card, which showed the previous address of R.R. #4, Lakefield, the writer had lettered the # symbol with a single cross-stroke as ++. And in the process of learning whether this idiosyncrasy would help to identify the writer, a still more important discovery was made. At about the time Provincial Constable Katz had been assigned to the case in January, Emmett Leahy's second son, Ralph, just turned twenty, had left home to find work in Edmonton, Alberta. He and his village girl friend were staying with friends in a trailer camp outside that city. Somehow Ralph had been overlooked; they had no specimen of his writing.

Ralph, as Detective Inspector Smith found, was not a frequent writer; the principal of the local school he had attended eventually had to be prevailed upon to root through hundreds of old exercise books before a verifiable specimen of his handwriting was obtained. It was enough. On March 23, the examiner at the Toronto Centre of Forensic Sciences made a tentative identification linking Ralph with the writing on the change-of-address card, and the following day Smith and Katz flew to Edmonton.

Ralph was out of work, and at home when they arrived at the trailer camp. At first he stubbornly denied any knowledge of the card. Smith asked him if he would object to writing out, from dictation, the wording on it. Just the wording, he said; not the signature at that point. Puzzled but seeing no danger, Ralph agreed. Smith let out the breath he had been holding; unconsciously, Ralph had drawn the exact duplicate of the single cross-stroke on the # symbol, and the tentative identification had become positive.

Abruptly, Ralph changed his story, as he was to do with dismal frequency in the next few months. He defiantly admitted writing and mailing the card, but produced a rambling explanation for doing so. On the day his uncle left for hospital, he said, he had been approached by a stranger who had

implied that he and Viola Leahy would be making off together, and offered Ralph fifty dollars to mail a card to the
post office after they had left. Ralph said he had eventually
consented, subject to payment in advance; the stranger had
duly met him later, and the money had been paid. It was, he
agreed, a strange episode; that was why he had not revealed
it before. But he was willing to take a lie-detector test if
Smith doubted his word. Again, the stubborn denial of any
additional knowledge.

Certain that Ralph was lying, Smith hoped that the youth
had sufficient intelligence to recognize the implausibility of
his story if given an interval for reflection. A confession would
save considerable time. But the next day found Ralph equally
determined to hold out; he had used the respite, in fact, only
to add some further detail. The man's first name was Harold.
His surname started with a *B*. His car was a black 1965
Dodge hardtop. He had not spoken to the man before, but he
had seen him in company with his aunt several times in the
previous few weeks.

With a sigh of resignation, Smith took down the details
of the man's description, and arrangements were made for a
police artist to produce a sketch. He knew how much time
and effort must be spent in a scrupulous search for a man in
whose existence he had no reason to believe, but it would
have to be done.

After arranging for Ralph Leahy to be kept under observation by the local force, Atholl Smith and Gary Katz returned to Peterborough with mixed feelings. He had secured
the youth's admission that he was responsible for the change-
of-address card and obtained a highly questionable explanation of why he had mailed it. But that was all. Ralph Leahy
had no known motive for harming his aunt, and for that matter, there was no proof of her death. Searches of the Leahy
farm made on foot, by a dog team and by helicopter had
brought no results.

A more personal concern was that Atholl Smith was

shortly due for a transfer to an administrative posting. The question was how the case could be advanced to a more positive stage before he handed it over without endangering the outcome by precipitate action.

The answer was not long in coming. At the beginning of April, the decision was made to issue a warrant for Ralph Leahy's arrest—on a charge of uttering a forged document. Ralph (who, as Smith had expected, had decided not to present himself for the polygraph test he had volunteered to take) was found hiding in a closet when Gary Katz arrived at the trailer to make the arrest, and by the night of April 5 was back in Peterborough. The following day, his father put up bail after his trial had been set for June 9.

It was an interesting case. Forgery had already been admitted, but in the absence of hard proof of an ulterior motive, it might appear a comparatively minor crime. The prosecution consequently wished the court to have knowledge of the suspicious circumstances in which the forgery had been committed as strongly as the defense wished to exclude them. Ralph Leahy's counsel accordingly contended that his client's plea of being guilty rendered further evidence unnecessary.

But this, to Atholl Smith's relief, Judge Collins was unwilling to accept out of hand. The Crown would be permitted to present the reasons for its objection, although no report of those reasons could be published unless, after proper consideration, he decided that the surrounding events were relevant to the charge. And after he had heard everything, and listened to the detective's description of the extensive search that had been made to locate any owner of a 1965 or 1966 Dodge (it was found the models were sufficiently similar to make a double check necessary) who fitted the description given by the accused, the judge gave his ruling. The evidence was relevant indeed; the only fact that could not be reported was Leahy's refusal to take a polygraph test, since he was under no obligation to agree.

The sentence was in accordance with the law; three months imprisonment, followed by two years on probation.

The disappearance of Viola Leahy remained to be solved, but Atholl Smith had the satisfaction of being able to take up his new posting with the knowledge that his four months of intensive work left the investigation in a much more advanced state than had seemed likely only a few weeks earlier.

Atholl Smith was succeeded on the case by Detective Inspector W. R. Perrin (now Superintendent Perrin, director of the OPP's Anti-Rackets Branch), who decided that Ralph Leahy's imprisonment in the Quinte Detention Centre at Napanee offered an opportunity to try a somewhat different approach to break down his sullen denial of any knowledge of his aunt's fate.

Ralph was due for release on August 9. On August 3, Perrin accordingly arranged for an undercover officer, not much older than Ralph but considerably more worldly and self-possessed in manner, to be admitted as a prisoner to the cell Ralph was sharing. The undercover man, incidentally, was also able to command a street vocabulary richer in color than Ralph's boringly repetitive farmyard obscenities.

It did not take the newcomer long to make the others aware he was into bigger time crime than anything they were likely to know about. He boasted confidently of the fix that was in, and that would have him sprung in a matter of days. Soon the conversation took a competitive turn; all wanted to proclaim their hardness and their criminal record. Ralph, who had only had minor brushes with the law and no previous convictions, spoke of seventeen break-ins and armed robberies he had taken part in, and claimed to have served two years in the slammer. Then he recklessly added that on his own release on August 9, he fully expected to be rearrested for murder and robbery.

Finding he had aroused the interest of his cellmates, he offered to elaborate. Just as he had done in Edmonton, however, he improvised a story that only partly implicated him, and seemed to glory in depicting himself as greedy, weak, and unreliable. He and a friend, he now said, had gone with a gun to rob his uncle's house when he was in hospital. Since he had been high on drugs at the time and had curled up for a nod at some point in the proceedings, he was not clear about all that had happened. But when he and his friend were dividing the $16,000 they had found in the couch, the friend said he had shot and killed Ralph's aunt.

"I didn't blame him, see. She'd had to die because she'd saw us. We was hoping the old bitch would drop dead when she saw the gun. So then," Ralph concluded, "I buried her."

The undercover man somehow managed to look at Ralph with an appropriate mixture of surprise, admiration and approval. "Well, lookit, kid," he said, "if they let you walk on Tuesday, mebbe I've got a proposition might interest you. I'll be staying at the Holiday Inn. How about looking me up on Wednesday?"

Ralph did not return to Lakefield on his release. His girlfriend had become pregnant in Edmonton, and arrangements had been made for them to occupy rooms in Peterborough. He celebrated their reunion by getting massively drunk which, he sheepishly explained when he presented himself the next day at the Holiday Inn, accounted for his swollen ankle and his hobble. He was warmly welcomed into the comfortable suite rented for the purpose which Detective Inspector Bill Perrin had, of course, already obtained authority to bug.

He spent most of that afternoon entranced, hearing of the exciting prospects of city crime and large payoffs. His new friend confided that he was a member of a highly organized automobile-theft gang stealing cars in Ontario and selling them in Quebec. Business was brisk, and they needed more drivers. The pay was four hundred dollars a run. Was Ralph interested?

Ralph certainly was; he only wanted to know when he could start. The undercover man laughed. It wasn't quite as easy as that, he explained. He recruited possible talent, but his boss had the final say. Ralph had already learned some-

thing about their operation. Once he was in, he would learn
much more, and the boss wouldn't permit that until he had at
least as much on Ralph as Ralph would have on him. Sure,
Ralph had told him a few things in the cell, but he was probably bullshitting. Now it was time for the straight goods, with
something they could check on.

Ralph talked, but stuck basically to the story he had told
in the detention center; nothing verifiable, much of it almost
certainly untrue, and all of it valueless in court. But Ralph
was a fish to be played carefully, although he had swallowed
the bait greedily. So the undercover man simply took notes,
gave him a drink and sent him on his way with the promise to
call him if the boss decided to hire him.

Ralph's repeated insistence that he had buried his aunt's
body somewhere on the farm in an area that had already
been searched was the least satisfactory part of the interview,
Bill Perrin thought as he listened to the recording. Even if he
was lying about the location, the whole farm seemed to have
been gone over thoroughly; Perrin had even persuaded Jim
Leahy to empty the few remaining feet of silage in the silo.
He had been hoping Ralph would have revealed the body
had been buried outside the farm, but the youth had sounded
both specific and convincing on that one point. In a final
effort to solve the disappearance scientifically, he arranged for
an infra-red photographic survey of the whole farm, but the
results continued to be unrewarding. They would have to
play their fish some more before they could land him.

On Friday, August 19, Ralph accordingly received a call
from his friend the recruiter at the Holiday Inn, who told him
to come there late that same evening. The timing was good.
Ralph was nearly penniless and despondent; nine days before
a rich future had seemed assured, but since then he had
heard nothing. Now his hopes revived.

But he found the atmosphere had chilled alarmingly. The
boss himself, large, loud and heavily bearded, was present
and in a bad humor. What kind of assholes did Ralph think

they were? So dumb they'd swallow any chicken shit he liked to feed them? Ralph had never been two years inside. He'd never been done for B and E. What Ralph was, the boss thought, was a police nark, and the boss's lot had things they liked to do with police narks. Ralph wouldn't be the first. And what was this crap about burying an aunt on his uncle's farm? The police had dug up the whole god damn farm months ago, and she wasn't there; the boss hàd good sources among that lot. Ralph might as well admit it; he had no idea where the old woman was.

Both afraid and indignant, Ralph offered to show them the actual body that night if they doubted him. The boss promptly said they were ready to call his bluff; that was exactly what he would have to do. They had forks and shovels in the car, and it was after midnight.

Arriving in Lakefield, Ralph led them without hesitation to a woody, swampy area to the southwestern corner of Jim Leahy's farm, not far from Emmett Leahy's house. After only a little thought, he indicated where they must dig. Meanwhile, of course, events were being observed from a distance by a surveillance unit. But their vigil was not rewarded. With Ralph near tears, the digging continued grimly until dawn. "But I buried her less'n a foot deep!" Ralph kept insisting.

The genuineness of his despair was so unmistakable that the undercover men were puzzled; Ralph believed his future with the car-theft ring, and possibly his own safety, depended on showing them a body he seemed to have lost. They drove him back to Peterborough in silence. Then the bearded man growled, "I don't know what to make of you, Ralph. You've wasted my night and shown me nothing. I can't be back here until next week. Meet me in the Holiday Inn next Thursday night, and I'll let you know what I've decided to do about you. But if we find you've been flanneling us, you're going to be in deep, deep trouble."

It was an empty threat made to see if it would stir Ralph into action of any significant kind, but he seemed to be dulled and defeated. Bill Perrin had to decide his own next move.

He had no doubt by now that Ralph was deeply implicated in his aunt's death, but did he have enough evidence for an arrest for murder? Although an identified body is not an essential for conviction—often enough the sheer circumstances of death make this impossible—its absence can make a jury uneasy, particularly if the motive is obscure. On the other hand, Ralph had already incriminated himself deeply, and it was all on tape. Was more to be gained by delaying longer, or by forcing the pace? He decided to act.

Ralph's next meeting with his prospective employers was made brief. They told him they had decided to try him out; they would let him know when his first run was to be carried out within the next few days. Then, after his subdued request for a fifty-dollar advance had been met, he was curtly dismissed.

His girl friend and one of his brothers were waiting for him in a car outside the hotel. As they drove away, another car cut them off. It held two of the team who had been keeping Ralph under constant observation. His brother was sent home, Ralph was arrested and the girl was taken in another car to be questioned by Detective Inspector Perrin.

Bill Perrin treated her gently. She had entered the eighth month of her pregnancy and was pitifully scared. It was apparent to him that behind the panicky lies and denials she started making was a confession of a secret that troubled her badly. Within minutes it came bursting from her; the previous November, Ralph had told her (grotesquely enough, at a local wedding) that he had done murder. At first she had thought he was joking. Later she had come to realize it was true, and he had confirmed that the victim had been his aunt. She asked tearfully, "Will I have to go to jail now?" Not if she had nothing to do with it, Perrin assured her.

At last Ralph Leahy faced the fact that further lying would not help him and decided he wanted as little publicity as possible to be given to the search for his aunt's body. The next day he directed the search to the same area he had dug before but still, even with daylight and more manpower, two days of effort brought nothing to light except some animal bones. Again Ralph became frantic. "Where are you, you old bitch?" he kept yelling. "You've never been anything but trouble to me."

By August 30, every square foot of exposed ground within the area Ralph had indicated to be the extreme limits of the site had been dug deep; hand-digging had failed. Now Perrin ordered in a large track power shovel.

They watched in fascination to see how effortlessly and smoothly the shovel dispassionately removed all growths, whether large or small, in the swampy area. For a long time nothing. Then, almost unbelievingly, they saw it swoop, skim lightly into the earth where a young willow was growing, daintily remove a woman's shoe, and toss it lightly at Perrin's feet. Willows, apparently, grow fast in swampy ground.

The machine was drawn back, and hand digging resumed. The body of Viola Leahy was lying below a tree only ten inches from the surface. She was still wearing the blue slacks, the multicolored blouse and the hand-knitted cardigan that she was wearing on the night of September 20 of the previous year. Beside her were her bifocal spectacles, unbroken. On her fingers were her rings. And in her body were still the bullets from the three shots, one penetrating the heart, that had been fired from the Marlin single-shot bolt-action .22 caliber rifle Ralph had already turned over to Perrin.

Decomposition was not sufficiently advanced as to make identification difficult, but it was carried out meticulously, even to a matching of fingerprints with those on Viola Leahy's medicine bottles in the bathroom. Her disappearance had ended.

The solution of the Leahy case, however, remains almost as puzzling as the disappearance had been. The investigation itself—the recognition of the symbol clue, the undercover gambit, the psychologically gauged appeal to Ralph Leahy's greed and vanity to coax him to talk, and the timing used to weaken his resistance—was an admirable combination of shrewd observation and guile. The final discovery of the body after so much frustrating and empty effort provides a moment of dramatic triumph. But then comes anti-climax: no further sensational disclosures, no logical resolution of loose ends and no clear motive. Just a senseless, unpremeditated killing of a harmless and rather pathetic old lady.

There was no evidence of material gain; her rings were untouched, and Ralph Leahy's prison boast of finding money in the couch seems totally untrue. Searching for motive, one of the detectives abruptly asked him if any other member of his family had had a part in the killing. He stared in bitter astonishment. ("Jim? My dad? Holy fuck, no. And my brothers aren't so stupid as to hang around with me.") The officers, who by then were able to class him as a poor and unconvincing liar however readily the lies came, judged that on this occasion he was hiding nothing.

And to the psychologists in the Oakridge Centre at Penetanguishene, Ralph Leahy also confirmed, flatly and without remorse, that he had acted alone; it was just that he had always hated his aunt, he said, and having thought of killing her for some time, suddenly saw his opportunity. What makes his actions still less comprehensible is that nobody recalled him expressing his hostility; his uncle was certain the two had always been on friendly terms. Nevertheless he was found fit to stand trial.

Even his account of the last hour of his aunt's existence is vexatiously incomplete. He recalled only bursting in on her that night with the gun, pointing it at her, and yelling, "Let's go!" Then he had marched her out to the barn, and shot her three times. He had returned the next day to bury her. There had to be more to it than that, though; there are the cigarette butts to be accounted for, the overturned flowerpot, and the disarranged couch. Presumably the command came as the climax to an angry, incoherent, and frightening scene which he was unwilling to reveal, and which we can only guess.

On February 24, 1978, Ralph Leahy was found guilty of non-capital murder, and was sentenced by Mr. Justice T. T. Callon to serve a sentence of sixteen years without parole. On appeal, on November 28, 1978, his sentence was reduced to ten years.

The sole expression of regret he ever voiced was to growl, after his arrest, "Whatever sentence they give me will be more than the old bitch was worth."

The Man Who Could Not Help Himself

The disappearance of Helen Robson Kendall, sometime during the week ending August 2, 1952, was not officially reported for about two weeks. Before the end of the month, the local police were not only convinced they had a case of foul play on their hands, but felt fairly sure the mystery would be solved and an arrest made as almost a routine procedure. Ultimately it proved to be a strange case which took more than nine years to bring to a conclusion, and made legal history.

At the time of her disappearance, Helen Kendall was thirty-three. Beginning eleven months after her marriage to Arthur James Kendall on her twentieth birthday, she bore five children. They ranged in age from Jimmy, then twelve, to the baby Mary, less than two. In between had come Margaret, close to eleven; Anne, even nearer to nine; and Jeannie, who was five and a half. Everyone describes Helen Kendall as a conscientious mother. If her dedication sometimes seemed joyless and even scolding, it would not be surprising; her married life had done little to encourage tranquillity. She was a fair-complexioned, angular woman, somewhat above average height, who walked with a slight limp. She had lived on farms all her life and dressed accordingly; it seems she usually wore a shabby old gray suit and scuffed brown orthopedic shoes.

Her occasional shrillness was her only defense against her husband's heavy-handed domination of his family. By all accounts, he was a capable worker when he chose to be, but a man incapable of making a steady success as a farmer. With his compact build, swarthy sensual looks and mocking eyes, there was a rogue-animal quality to Arthur Kendall. He had been in trouble off and on since his youth, and wherever he went, cautious neighbors had learned to be wary of dealings with him. Their sons, however, were likelier to admire his spirit, his wiles and the total freedom from guilt he seemed to possess.

At the age of forty-two, he was still nominally a farmer, owning a hundred acres of farmland in Monkton, in south-western Ontario, which he had purchased in 1946. When his barn burned down in 1950—suffering the same fate as the barns on two of his earlier farms—he did not replace it. Instead, he applied $3,500 of the insurance settlement to secure clear title to the whole farm preparatory to offering it for resale. It left him with a balance of $4,000.

In the spring of 1952, with time heavy on his hands, he earned a little money by helping to sow a flax crop on a farm in Lakeside, thirty or so miles to the south. The work completed, he traded in his 1937 Plymouth on a 1951 Ford and told his family he proposed taking off on a fishing trip up on the Bruce Peninsula.

Clearly, he was a man who acted on impulse. He had driven up the peninsula until he had almost reached its peak at Tobermory, where the toll ferry takes passengers to Manitoulin Island, when he chanced to meet Ashford Pedwell, the owner of a local sawmill. This was on the Lake Huron side of the peninsula at a place, too small to be shown on most maps, called Johnston's Harbour. Pedwell told him he also owned some land there, on which he wanted flax planted; more than one man would be needed for the job, and he could find no local help. He needed help in the sawmill, too. There was a cabin nearby in which to live.

Kendall decided to accept and undertook to find helpers. He told Pedwell he himself would be willing to work for him until September, and immediately started calling some of the young men he knew in Monkton, all farmers' sons, who might fancy a paid vacation in his company for a few weeks in exchange for some hours of work each day.

One accepted promptly, and traveled up that weekend to start work with Kendall on Monday, May 26. He was to stay until the latter part of June. Two others also accepted, but could only get away from their fathers' farms to work the second two weeks of June and July.

So far as Pedwell was concerned, the work went smoothly. For his temporary employees, the work afforded a pleasant background in a primitive setting for an all-male party, particularly when the full group was assembled in the latter part of June. On one of their evening jaunts they decided to take a meal at an eating place in Wiarton called the Olympia restaurant, where they were served by an attractive waitress called Bea.

Bea was Beatrice Hogue. At thirty-seven she was as vivid and lushly female as Helen Kendall, four years younger, was defensive and withdrawn. Bea, moreover, evidently throve on the procreative process; she had a daughter and son aged sixteen and fifteen from a first marriage which had ended with her husband's sudden death, and had six surviving children by the second. Just now, however, she was by way of being a free agent. Her husband worked on ships sailing the Great Lakes and had not been home for some months.

It is extremely doubtful whether, at their first meeting in the Olympia restaurant, Beatrice Hogue or Art Kendall sensed much beyond the certainty that he would be sharing her bed that night as a matter of mutual gratification. Both were full-blooded creatures who had been deprived of sex for longer than was comfortable. Kendall, somebody said, was "sexy as a Jersey bull, and Beatrice Hogue was just the woman to cope with such a man."

Kendall apparently had no suspicion of how fully involved with Bea he was to become. Full of unaccustomed good humor, he telephoned Helen to say that at the beginning of July (when his young companions had gone home and school would be out), he would drive down to Monkton to pick up the family so that they could all spend summer together in the cabin.

Until the end of June a bacchanalian mood seems to have prevailed at the Hogue home in Wiarton. Kendall's young companions may sometimes have been invited to join, and one or more members of Bea's family may also have been included. Art Kendall's interest in Bea became less casual. An elderly neighbor, an early riser with a keen interest in local activities, regularly observed Art's new Ford outside the Hogue home overnight, and saw Kendall driving off to the sawmill soon after six in the morning.

Just as Arthur had promised, he drove down to his Monkton farmhouse at the beginning of July and returned to the cabin with Helen and all the children. Perhaps Beatrice had warned him that her husband, Tom Hogue, was expected back during the month. Possibly Kendall himself had decided the time had come for a month of family life to avoid becoming too deeply involved. Possibly his wife announced she would bring the family up to Johnston's Harbour anyway, even if he failed to keep his promise. Many suppositions are possible.

What is certain is that the five children and their parents became the occupants of the tiered bunks in the primitive twelve-foot-by-fourteen-foot cabin, four and a half miles from the nearest highway through the bush country—and that Art Kendall found it impossible to break off his affair with Beatrice Hogue. When Tom Hogue presented himself at his own doorstep in Wiarton on July 12, Bea turned him away.

Did Beatrice know of the existence of Helen Kendall tucked away in the cabin about forty miles to the north of Wiarton? Beatrice did not say; Kendall later indicated that the question had not arisen. Independent witnesses stated that Kendall, from the time he had met Beatrice Hogue, told several people that he was a widower. (Nothing especially sinister in that, of course. In that age, when divorce would have sounded odder as an explanation, many married men enjoying a solo vacation probably claimed to be widowers. Awkward, certainly, if the wife suddenly appears, but the cabin was out in the wilds, and Helen Kendall was no gadabout.)

Whatever Art Kendall represented himself to be to the outside world, however, there was no chance that he could expect his wife to remain ignorant of the time he was spending with another woman. This was not a new situation in their lives by any means. Kendall's unbridled sexual drive was something of a local legend, and it was a matter of fairly common knowledge that after the birth of her fifth child, Helen Kendall had told him to stay away from her unless he would submit to a vasectomy. To be deprived of fruitful seed was the worst humiliation he could imagine.

It is easy to imagine the old arguments being renewed each time Kendall returned to the cabin. Now there were probably two new themes, Helen's isolation from everyone she knew, and Art's neglect of his own children on vacation. In turn, Helen would be asked what right she had, a woman ashamed of motherhood, to talk about the way a parent should behave. Sometime in July, she wrote to her mother in Brantford to say that she proposed to return with the children to Monkton about the time of the August first holiday weekend. Whether she told her mother or not, one thing was evident. The vacation was not a success.

Promptly at seven o'clock on the morning of Saturday, August 2, 1952, Art Kendall reported as usual at the Pedwell farm, and worked steadily until four. He then returned to the cabin and told the elder children to pack everything up and clear it out. Putting them all in the car together with the family baggage, he set off for Wiarton. Helen Kendall was not with them, but for reasons that were then obscure, their mother's absence was no surprise to the children. Arriving at the Hogue house, Kendall ushered them inside, nonchalantly remarking, "Beatrice, this is my family," before striding off to the bathroom to shave. They were left to introduce themselves to Beatrice Hogue and the six of her own children who still lived with her. A new domestic life had started.

The following Monday, August 4, was a holiday, but Ashford Pedwell went to his office as usual. On the door he found a note reading:

> The flax is ready to go and I have family troubles and have to leave. I simply cannot help myself.
>
>   Yours, Arthur Kendall

Details of the unusual caravan that made its way from Wiarton down to Monkton are scarce. We know that the next time Tom Hogue returned to his house he found Beatrice had stripped it clean. It is reasonable, then, to suppose that not only Arthur Kendall and his five children, together with Beatrice Hogue and her six children, but much of the Hogue household furnishings made the passage. It was observed by one of Kendall's neighbors in Monkton, a farmer by the name of Jim Broughton who knew enough about Kendall's nature to feel a considerable sympathy for Helen Kendall.

He was puzzled enough by what he had seen to make a visit to the Kendall farmhouse and was amazed to see that "a strange woman and a whole lot of strange children" were now sharing it. There was no visible sign of Helen Kendall. Concerned, he asked Art where she was. Well, they had had a tiff, he was told; his wife had ended it by hitting him with a teacup, he had gone for a drive to cool down, and when he had returned, the children told him their mother had packed up her few things and taken off on foot. Beatrice Hogue was a married lady who, taking pity on his children's predicament, had consented to look after them until their mother returned. Jim Broughton left, far from satisfied, feeling it was quite unlike Helen Kendall to leave her children by themselves; still less, to allow another woman to look after them.

Broughton accordingly returned to the Kendall farm the next Monday, August 11. The situation had not changed ex-

cept that Kendall said that he now knew that Helen was staying with her mother and her brother on the family farm at
Brantford. This was something that could be verified, and
since he was acquainted with the family, he rang them as
soon as he had returned home. He heard what he had been
afraid of hearing; her family had not heard from Helen since
the card she had sent in July and knew nothing of her whereabouts. Thoroughly alarmed, Jim Broughton promptly
notified the Sebringville detachment of the Ontario Provincial
Police that Helen Kendall was missing. This was the first time
that her disappearance had been officially reported.

The Sebringville OPP were to receive a second report
about Helen Kendall in the early hours of the next morning.
As soon as he had heard the substance of Jim Broughton's
phone call, Helen's elder brother, Ross Cameron, who had
managed the family farm since their father's death, drove
from Brantford to the Monkton farm, arriving after dark. It
was a stormy and unproductive meeting which apparently reduced Kendall to tearful denials. Among Kendall's characteristics, two of the most interesting are his reliance on his ingenuity to improvise a solution from any problem arising out
of his more reckless actions, and an ability to unleash floods
of staggeringly romanticized emotions depicting himself as an
ill-used victim. Signs of immaturity, perhaps, but they undeniably gave him a long run. Ross Cameron, however, knew
him too well and took his suspicions to Sebringville.

Early on Tuesday, the official investigation started.
OPP officers from the nearest points went to Johnston's Harbour to interview Ashford Pedwell and the owners of the
store who had known Helen Kendall; to Wiarton to talk to
Beatrice Hogue's neighbors; and to Monkton to interview the
farmers' sons who had been Art Kendall's companions, and to
take a statement from Kendall himself.

Kendall repeated the same story he had told his brother-
in-law with a few embellishments. He had, he said, come
home dog-tired at six in the evening of Thursday, July 31, and
found his wife had made no move to prepare the evening

meal for the family. She was in one of her frequent tempers. He had done what he could to reason with her, but her scolding had only grown worse. At half past eight had come the assault with the empty teacup (this semiludicrous teacup incident is a recurrent motif in so many subsequent relations of the quarrel that it almost certainly happened at some time), and he had been so upset that he slammed out of the door, and entered his car.

He went on to say that he had driven as far as Wiarton and entered the Olympia restaurant, where Beatrice Hogue worked, to get something to eat. But he had been too worried by his wife's outburst to enjoy food, and he had been pacing the streets of Wiarton until three in the morning. Then, since he knew he must get some sleep before starting his day's work, he drove back to the cabin. But when he arrived, his wife had gone. In the morning his children had told him how she had packed her few possessions into a shopping bag soon after his own departure, and walked out.

Yes, he had to agree, before his wife could reach the highway she would have to make her way along a lonely trail through four miles of bush populated by bears and rattlesnakes; she did walk with some difficulty; and, yes, at that time of the evening the light would be dwindling. He could only say that showed just how mad she must have been. Although it had all happened twelve days ago, he had not reported the matter because, until his brother-in-law had told him otherwise last night, he was sure she had been at Brantford.

A statement obtained from the storekeeper's wife in Johnston's Harbour, however, did not tally with this account at all. The lady had become quite friendly with Helen Kendall during her month's stay, and clearly remembered seeing her, untroubled and in good spirits, when she had come in to do some shopping quite late on the Thursday evening Art claimed she left him. In fact, she was fairly sure she had also seen Helen Kendall the next day as well, although she could not swear to it.

At that point it began to look as if it would be a relatively straightforward case. Helen Kendall had been alive and in good spirits on Thursday and was missing by Saturday when Arthur Kendall had written his note to Ashford Pedwell. There was no trace of Helen Kendall leaving Johnston's Point. Her mother and brother in Brantford, with whom she would almost certainly try to communicate, had neither seen her nor heard from her. The possibility of foul play, suicide or accident was so strong that the early discovery of the body in some nearby spot seemed predictable.

At first it seemed as if fate might be offering an assist to the provincial police and their investigation. The day following Kendall's statement, his nearly new 1951 Ford, on which he had made no payments since its purchase in May, was repossessed by the finance company, which might limit his mobility, and made it more certain that Kendall would present himself for a further interview, as he had promised, in the OPP offices August 18. He came—but this time he was accompanied by a lawyer. Much as he wanted the mystery of his wife's whereabouts to be solved, he said, his lawyer had advised him to say nothing. The lawyer nodded his agreement. That was as far as the OPP could get.

Two days later, despite the loss of his automobile, Kendall left Monkton. Somehow he found a way to transpose his enlarged family in its entirety to Lakeside to harvest the crop of flax he had helped to plant in May; somehow he prevailed on the Lakeside farmer to accommodate them all; and somehow the farmer had been persuaded to allow Kendall and his "housekeeper," Beatrice Hogue, to share the double bedroom on the main floor.

Kendall's departure did not go unnoticed, however, and the following day two OPP officers visited the Lakeside farm unannounced to take a further statement. This proved impossible. Kendall and Beatrice Hogue had borrowed the farmer's pickup truck to collect the mail from Wiarton. Likely too, they wanted to bring down whatever remained of the Hogue household possessions.

This temporary absence provided the first opportunity the police had had to talk to the three elder children. Jimmy, Margaret, and Anne all sat in the police cruiser, and in frightened little voices, never once looking the officers in the face, muttered a brief confirmation of their father's story. They were, both men sensed, wildly resolved not to depart from an invisible text or enlarge on it in any way. Their fright convinced their listeners, as fully as the most damning evidence could have done, that their mother was dead, but they recognized the possible danger of questioning them more thoroughly.

The officers had another thought. Kendall's Ford having been repossessed, an expert examination could be made of its trunk and its interior for traces of bloodstains or other indications that it had once carried a dead or dying woman. But the closest scrutiny brought the case no nearer to a solution.

Fresh hopes were aroused on September 3, when a cardboard box was found hidden in a bush about a mile from the cabin. It contained female clothing and a copy of the July 12 issue of the *Farmer's Advocate* addressed to Arthur Kendall and forwarded from Monkton. Smears on the magazine cover, moreover, looked as if they might be bloodstains.

Kendall was interviewed again in the children's presence. They all identified the clothing as an old sundress belonging to Helen Kendall, but the children said it was not what she had been wearing when she had walked out of the cabin. And when the report came back from the laboratory, the stains could not be positively identified as human blood. The certainty the police felt that Kendall and his children knew more than they admitted about Helen Kendall's disappearance was further strengthened, but the final link was still missing.

Inspector Harold Graham was dispatched from the OPP Criminal Investigation Branch in Toronto to help the widespread team of officers now on the case. A further development was reported when a witness was found who said he had seen Kendall hiding a shovel just off a side road at a spot two and a half miles north of his farm. At the approach of an automobile, Kendall had ducked for cover. A second witness, unacquainted with the first and unaware of his statement, reported that Kendall had asked to be driven to the same location at a later time, and that he had seen Kendall rescue a shovel.

Significant evidence, although Kendall flatly denied that either incident had occurred. Meeting Kendall for the first time, Inspector Graham was certain that he was more uneasy when questioned about the shovel than on any other point. But what was it evidence of, by itself, however strong the proof? A close search of the farm area had revealed nothing, nor did it seem probable that the body had been removed from the Bruce Peninsula.

Up at Johnston's Harbour, Inspector Graham organized a more massive search. Fifteen police officers and twenty-five members of the public made a two-day foot-by-foot examination along the entire length of the Johnston's Harbour Road for a hundred yards on either side. Still nothing.

The weeks went by. The flax-cutting in Lakeside was completed in mid-September, and the combined Kendall-Hogue household returned to Monkton. In October Kendall found a buyer for his farm; the sale was closed on October 19, and the troupe moved on again. Kendall had presumably had enough of the worries and responsibilities of land-ownership; the department of the provincial fire marshal was also becoming inquisitive about the three barn-burnings he had sustained. Henceforward he would work for others when it suited him; he was indisputably skilled and strong enough to find employment without much difficulty. Wherever he went, Beatrice Hogue and the household moved with him. So, too, did the eyes of the local police.

On the Bruce Peninsula, the hope remained that the influx of hunters for the annual fall deer-hunt in the four townships north of Wiarton would turn up some trace previously missed, but nothing was reported. Only one possibility seemed left. At quite a short distance from the cabin was a floating marsh; a body deposited in it would be lost forever.

This was a possibility the police had to face, dispiriting as it was. Without a body or evidence of violence, whatever fate had befallen Helen Kendall might remain undetected. If Arthur Kendall was accountable for his wife's disappearance, as they strongly suspected, the OPP accordingly had an even greater responsibility to watch his future behavior with particular care.

Perhaps it was in consequence that in the second week of January 1953, Provincial Constable Outingdyke (an officer who had already played an active part in the investigation and later became an extremely efficient probation officer) arrested Kendall for a vicious beating he had given his elder daughter Margaret for stopping at a neighbor's house on her way home from school. The scene had been witnessed, and the girl had required medical attention, but she swore in court that her injury was caused by a fall on the ice and her father was acquitted. A week later, however, evidence given before the Family Relation Board concerning life in the Kendall-Hogue household resulted in the Children's Aid Society in Stratford being awarded a six-month temporary wardship of the Kendall children and one-year wardship of the Hogue children. Interestingly enough, the most conclusive evidence was provided by two of the Monkton farmers' sons who had been Arthur Kendall's companions up at Johnston's Harbour.

Inspector Graham of the Criminal Investigation Branch followed all these developments with interest. He was sure a break in the case would come, but he knew it would not solve itself automatically. He made a point of knowing Kendall's whereabouts and of dropping in on him unannounced from time to time to take a further statement; officially, for the purpose of clearing up some query; unofficially, to watch for slips, contradictions and signs of uncertainty.

Kendall responded to the challenge with pious invention. The night he had previously claimed he spent pacing the streets of Wiarton in despair at his wife's ill temper was, he now tearfully revealed, occupied in a suicide attempt. He had bled the brakes on his car, and he had driven at a hundred miles an hour to Tobermory, intending to drive off the pier so his family could benefit from his life insurance policy. "But I hadn't counted on finding seventy cars lined up on the pier, blocking my way. It was God's own intervention to save me from sin," he said sanctimoniously.

On another occasion his mother, aged eighty, was with him. Both insisted that Helen Kendall was alive and well. Inspector Graham mildly inquired where they thought the police should look for her. Old Mrs. Kendall was certain she would be found doing the only work she ever seemed capable of doing reasonably well—baking bread. Arthur Kendall reproved his mother. "You're forgetting the beautiful voice she has. Take my word, you'll find her in a foreign opera house. She'll be a star, singing under an Italian name."

Yet another time, Kendall begged for Graham's indulgence; Beatrice Hogue, he said, was suffering from cancer, and the doctor had told him to expect her death within two weeks. Arthur Kendall, clearly, was never dull company.

Graham had an ulterior purpose to serve with his visits. They allowed him to become better acquainted with Kendall's elder children as they were growing up, and make them gradually aware they could look to him as a friend who had no intention of persecuting them.

Years had now gone by. In July 1959 Margaret Kendall, eighteen, left the Kendall household to marry and live in another province. In December of that year, on Arthur Kendall's application, a judge in Goderich issued an order declaring Helen Kendall, whom her husband had neither seen nor heard from "since on or about July 29, 1952," to be presumed dead under the appropriate section of the Marriage Act. On March 26, 1960, Arthur Kendall, widower, and Beatrice Hogue, divorced wife of Thomas Hogue (he had instituted divorce proceedings in 1952), were married at Camlachie, Ontario. In November 1960 Kendall's second daughter, Anne, now seventeen, also left home.

On January 20, 1961, it was Anne who came to Inspector

Top right: Mrs. Viola Leahy ("All a Green Willow Is My Garland") Courtesy of the Ontario Provincial Police

Top left: Ralph Leahy. It was just that he always hated his aunt. ("All a Green Willow Is My Garland") Courtesy of the Ontario Provincial Police

Middle: The discovery of Viola Leahy's body in the willow patch. ("All a Green Willow Is My Garland") Courtesy of the Ontario Provincial Police

Bottom: The telltale change-of-address card mailed by Ralph Leahy. ("All a Green Willow Is My Garland")

Top: The Kendall family in a snapshot probably taken in 1949. ("The Man Who Could Not Help Himself") Copyright, Canapress Photo

Bottom: Arthur Kendall at the time of his trial, 1961. ("The Man Who Could Not Help Himself") Courtesy of the Ontario Provincial Police

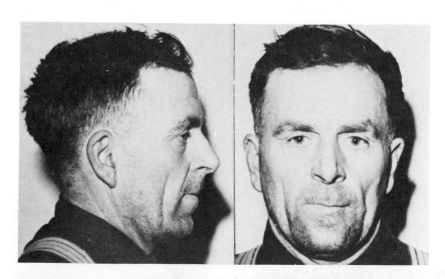

Clifford Robert Olson ("Runaways, Ramblers, and Rascals") Copyright, Canapress Photo

Side: Fred Johnsen. Speculations over the reasons for Johnsen's "kidnapping" are as numerous as the rumors. ("Unusual Disturbance in Forest Hill") Copyright, Canapress Photo

Bottom: Frederick Johnsen's Forest Hill home. Mr. and Mrs. Youcef Debabi and child are shown in the foreground on the day following Fred Johnsen's disappearance. ("Unusual Disturbance in Forest Hill") Copyright, reproduced by kind permission of The Globe and Mail, *Toronto.*

Harold Graham and made the voluntary statement he had felt
would one day be forthcoming.

How much reliance would be placed on the testimony of
a seventeen-year-old girl of her recollection of events that had
occurred when she was not quite nine years old? Graham
asked her to draw a diagram of the cabin from memory, indicating the position of the bunks, the window, table, stove
and door. Her memory was surprisingly accurate. But one
child's testimony might not be enough if contradicted by the
two elder children.

Anne's sister Margaret was interviewed in her own home
in another province and independently asked whether, since
Anne had already made a statement to Inspector Graham, she
was willing to give her own recollections of what had really
happened in that cabin on the morning of Saturday, August 2,
1952. With only minor variations, Margaret told the same
story.

As both girls had expected, their brother James, although
now on the verge of his twentieth birthday but still living at
home under his father's domination, still refused to speak. It
was not necessary. Arthur Kendall, then working as a day laborer, was arrested and charged with the murder of his wife,
Helen Kendall, when he arrived for work at the Clinton Air
School on the R.C.A.F. base at Clinton, Ontario, on the morning of January 27, 1961.

The memory the children had had to contain for nearly
half their lives was still vivid in their minds. Anne and
Margaret had been sleeping in the bunks over those of their
parents. At dawn on the Saturday morning, they had been
awakened by their mother's screams. They both quoted her
words: "Don't, Art! Oh, please don't!" A minute later, they
had seen their father place a bloody butcher's knife on the
cabin table. Then there was the remembered vision of him
dragging their mother's limp body out of the door.

Another memory of a terrible silent wait of possibly
twenty minutes before he returned. In silence, he had me-

thodically set to work wiping up blood from the floor with bed sheets, pillow slips and their mother's clothing. Finished at last, he had bundled up the knife in the bloodstained clothing and bedding, and again departed for what seemed about the same length of time. Back once more, he had methodically scrubbed the floor and then commanded the elder girl, Margaret, to follow him outside.

Margaret went on to say that, doing exactly as he told her, she entered the front seat of the Ford and was driven to a fork in the road where her father had stopped the car. Fiercely, he had told her the story of the Thursday night quarrel and of her mother's voluntary departure the same night after he had left; that, he growled menacingly, was what Margaret must always tell everyone, and that was what Margaret must be sure to see her brother and her sisters learned to tell everyone forever and ever.

The children knew that their father was not a man to disobey. That was the whole story. It was not until more than eleven weeks after his two sisters had made their statements that James could bring himself to believe that whether he remained silent or not, and even though his mother's body might never be found, his father could be found guilty of her murder. On April 14, he hesitantly gave a signed statement confirming the truth of the girls' testimony, adding that he did so although he was still in fear for his sisters' safety—and now for his own.

This was said to be the first Canadian murder trial without an identified corpse to provide evidence of a crime. Clearly, however, if sufficient corroborative evidence can be presented, a killer cannot escape retribution simply by finding a way to make recovery of his victim's body impossible; there are ample precedents in English, American and Australian courts of convictions obtained where the *corpus delicti* has consisted of unassailable verbal testimony.

The Kendall case certainly made Canadian legal history in another way, since it was the first in which a charge of capital murder was brought after the parliamentary decision to distinguish between "capital" murder, to which the death penalty then automatically applied, and unpremeditated or "non-capital" murder. It was also notable as being the first case to be tried by Mr. Justice W. D. Parker after his appointment.

The trial itself, which opened at Walkerton on October 23, 1961, was not lengthy. The defense was basically an attempt to depict the scene that the children had witnessed in the cabin as the unintended and unpremeditated sequel to a stormy domestic argument following Kendall's return at daybreak after a night of illicit lovemaking. The jury, unconvinced, returned a verdict of guilty as charged after two hours deliberation on October 27.

The hush in court was broken by the loud sobbing of Beatrice Kendall. Her husband of little more than a year remained calm and quietly said some words of meaningless reassurance to her in a gentle tone probably unfamiliar to his own children. The judge then instructed the jury to retire again, and then report whether they wished to add a recommendation for executive clemency.

They duly withdrew, coming back in five minutes to confirm that was their wish. Then, as he was required to do, the judge declared the solemn sentence of death.

Kendall did not give up lightly. When his appeal against this sentence was rejected by the Ontario Court of Appeal, he took it to the Supreme Court of Canada which, too, upheld the sentence. Before it was carried out, however, executive clemency was exercised, and the sentence was commuted to life imprisonment.

One interesting aspect of the case is the extraordinary mutual biological attraction between two such prolific, almost insatiable, breeders as Arthur Kendall and Beatrice Hogue. Even more remarkable is the bitter irony of their union. She became pregnant by him four times: she suffered a miscarriage in 1954; a child born on July 1, 1956 died three days later; stillborn children were delivered on October 25, 1957 and on January 13, 1960.

This succession of misfortunes proved to be caused by Beatrice Hogue's blood type being Rh negative, while Kendall's was normal Rh positive. Quite certainly, Thomas Hogue—by whom she had had six surviving children—must have been Rh negative (a condition shared by only some 15 percent of the population), and there is a strong possibility that her first husband, Horace Hooey, may also have been Rh negative.

Arthur Kendall was sent to serve life imprisonment in the New Westminster Penitentiary in British Columbia. Beatrice Kendall moved to live near the penitentiary in order to see him whenever visiting hours allowed. In 1971, working on the prison farm, he made an escape. He was recaptured the next day, enjoying his wife's company; he offered no resistance to his captors, and was said to be smiling happily. After being paroled, he rejoined her in 1975.

The children's account of the blood that had to be first mopped and then scrubbed from the cabin floor may make it seem surprising that scientific evidence could not be presented to confirm their statements. Indeed, biologists from the provincial Attorney General's laboratory did find bloodstains on the floor between the bunk and the cabin door—but, alas, this was not until January 25, 1961, after the girl's statements had been given. Molecular changes that occur in bloodstains over a period of years make positive identification of human blood impossible.

Inspector Harold Graham of the OPP Criminal Investigation Branch, whose patient determination was a major factor in bringing Arthur Kendall to trial, later became Commissioner of the OPP until his retirement in 1981. He always deprecated any attempt to depicit him as the hero of the case, stressing that the investigation was a team effort owing its success mainly to the dedication and initiative of the men in the field. It would have been impossible without them, of course, but not unjustifiably the disappearance of Helen Kendall came to be known, with a certain affection, as "the Commissioner's case."

Runaways, Ramblers
and Rascals

When a child of ten or less is missing for more than a day, it is unlikely to be from the child's own choice. In the second half of childhood the reverse is true, particularly between the ages of eleven and fourteen when the child is dealing with emerging sexuality. Girls respond rather more impulsively than boys; an analysis of figures for missing juveniles in that age group shows the girls outnumbering the boys by a ratio of about five to four. The combined totals for the next age group from fifteen up are not so high, and the male component is still lower; the ratio of girls to boys increases to more than five to three.

Without accurate figures for the earlier part of the century, it is impossible to make a direct comparison, but nobody seems to doubt that the incidence of the runaway teenager and pre-teenager has increased more rapidly in the past twenty years than over the preceding sixty or so years. The other big difference is that the earlier runaway was much likelier to be a boy than a girl.

Why do they leave? Secret departures out of shame or fear of the consequences of a soon-to-be-discovered indiscretion are much less frequent today than in midcentury Canada. More sensible and less drastic alternatives are now available, but some still occur, particularly among first-generation

Canadian families. Considerably more teenagers leave home in open defiance of their parents than two generations ago. Some will keep in touch. Others disappear from sight.

Some are rebelling against families that are too strict, some are in search of adventure, excitement or a chance to discover their own potential. Many have no clear goal, but are simply trying to escape a sordid home atmosphere. Such children usually follow a repetitive pattern of attempted flight from home. Psychiatrists describe it as a runaway reaction.

Dr. Selwyn M. Smith, associate professor at the University of Ottawa and psychiatrist-in-chief at the Royal Ottawa Hospital, has seen enough cases to be able to describe the usual background and outline the profile of the child concerned. The girl or boy, he says, is generally an only child, unwanted and resented from the time of conception, likely to be immature and timid. Most are loners, some associate with delinquent gangs, but never as leaders and always on the fringe, largely ignored. Unable to express aggression directly, inadequate and friendless, their inner anger and frustration takes devious forms in the home; sly thefts, petty deceits, mainly unexplained absences. At first for a night. Later, for longer periods. One day, perhaps, permanently.

The repeated departures and returns mean that some months may have gone by without either direct or indirect news of the child before notice is taken of the disappearance. In some homes, there will be little eagerness to have the absence reported or for the child to be found. The child may drift into the sub-culture of drug dealing and part-time hooking on the streets of some big city, near or distant. In Dr. Selwyn Smith's experience, a youthful male runaway's persistent inability to assert himself, coupled with his unsatisfied hunger for acceptance, can lead to passive homosexual experience.

For the police, runaways who are over the age at which they are considered juveniles in their province (sixteen, seventeen or eighteen, as the case may be) must be treated as free agents. In most big cities, private agencies exist which can help parents actively concerned for a daughter's or son's welfare, usually on a fee basis.

The police are not always informed that a previously reported disappearance has been ended; many cases might remain officially unsolved if the police did not keep in touch with families at regular intervals. The reluctance to reveal family problems to outsiders that frequently delays the reporting of a disappearance often applies more forcibly to the reappearance. Understandable enough, if the family considers the matter closed, the police seldom wish to pry further.

Teenage runaways still classified as juveniles, and whose absence has been officially reported, are frequently found by the police as a result of their own street activities bringing them to official notice. Many persistent juvenile runaways are located in the same way, although their parents have never reported them missing. In these cases, the behavior is almost certain to be repeated no matter whether the persistent runaway is returned to the parents, entrusted to goodhearted foster parents or provided with psychiatric treatment and professional care. Freedom to run has become an imperative. Any form of restriction, however gentle, is regarded as being harsh and punitive. In a tragic sense, they are doomed to remain lost even at those times their whereabouts is known.

Although the number of persistent runaways with severe psychic pathology can be taken as an index of the times, they form a minority of the total. In many cases, the runaway returns to the family circle and, in the course of time, the incident is only something to be remembered occasionally with a wry smile.

Clearly, not all the young people who disappear do so from choice. It cannot be ignored that they are likely to be attractive and vulnerable targets for unsought attention.

Cases of disappearances attributable to multiple murderers of adolescents and young adults are recorded worldwide throughout criminal history, although in the first part of this century in the western world most found their victims among the seamiest and most transient sections of the community, or during times of war or disorder.

The German youth-murderer Fritz Haarman who, in Hanover after the First World War, sold the flesh of his victims in the meat market, was active for five years; a list of twenty-eight teenage victims was produced at his trial, but the true total is thought to exceed fifty.

In more recent years, the increasing number of unaccompanied young vacationers and travelers through thinly populated, lonely parts has increased their opportunities.

Ian Brady and Myra Hindley, known as the Moors Murderers, were arrested in England in 1966 after the discovery of the body of a recently killed teenage homosexual, but were found to have been responsible for the murder of a ten-year-old girl who had disappeared eleven months earlier and of a twelve-year-old boy missing two years. Both had been tortured and their bodies buried in the moors north of Manchester.

In Houston, Texas, Dean Corll had two teenage pimps working to satisfy his tastes for rape, strangulation and mutilation of young boys. His crimes remained undiscovered until one of his pimps shot and killed him in 1973.

The Chicago building contractor John Gacy buried his thirty-two victims on his own grounds; they were all teenage male prostitutes. He was active for several years before his arrest in 1978.

Outwardly, the offenders have little in common. Some are otherwise law-abiding, others have a long criminal record. Some live alone, others are married with families. Some are in their twenties, thirties and forties. Albert Fish of Westchester County, New York, was fifty-eight. Described in a case study written by the court-appointed psychiatrist, Dr. Frederick Wertham, Fish was said to be "like a meek and innocuous little old man . . . If you wanted to entrust your children to someone, he would be the one you would choose." Fish however was thought to have been responsible for many child murders over several decades. Some, on the other hand, have a record of violence and look like it.

On January 14, 1982, a forty-two-year-old construction worker named Clifford Robert Olson pleaded guilty in the B. C. Supreme Court in Vancouver to eleven charges of murder—eight girls ranging in age from twelve to eighteen, and three boys of nine, fifteen and sixteen. Not victims from the half-world of sex and crime, but innocent and guileless youngsters from respectable homes.

The first victim, a twelve-year-old girl, had been stabbed to death on November 17, 1980, but her body was not discovered until that Christmas Day. Early in January 1981 Olson was arrested for a different offense committed on New Year's Day (which happened to be his birthday) involving rape, buggery, indecent assault and possession of a gun. It had only been 123 days since his last imprisonment; most of the days that had passed since he was seventeen had, in fact, been spent serving time for offenses that included breaking and entering, theft, forgery and false pretenses, armed robbery and escaping from custody. The next murder, the bludgeoning of a thirteen-year-old girl, was committed on April 16, 1981, only eight days after he had been released on bail to await trial for the New Year's Day offense.

Five days later he beat a sixteen-year-old boy to death; about the same date, his son was born. On May 15, he married the child's mother, and four days later bludgeoned a sixteen-year-old girl to death. A week later he was charged with drunk driving and contributing to juvenile delinquency following an accident in which he was suspiciously involved with a fifteen-year-old girl he had picked up. June proved an almost uneventful month marked only by the strangling of a thirteen-year-old girl, but a busier month was coming.

On July 2, he strangled a nine-year-old boy, and on July 7, a sixteen-year-old girl laid a charge of indecent assault against him. Avoiding arrest, he stabbed a fourteen-year-old girl to death two days later, and the following day drove off for an eleven-day vacation in the United States. In the remaining ten days of the month, he bludgeoned a fifteen-year-old boy to death, beat to death one girl of eighteen and

one of seventeen, and strangled one of fifteen. He then took
off for a week in Calgary. It would prove his last month of
freedom, but he was not taken into custody until August 12,
when the police feared for the lives of the two girl hitchhikers
he had picked up. On August 18, he was told that he would
be charged with the murder of the one girl they had evidence
of his meeting.

The case is too recent to require extensive review for Canadian readers, and at the time this is being written it is far
from certain that no further disclosures can be expected.
Olson has reportedly spoken of having knowledge concerning
twenty-eight other unsolved murders without indicating
whether or not he had committed them himself. He remains a
suspect in another child-killing in the summer of 1981 which
he has not admitted and, since it is not easy to believe that he
never engaged in this extreme form of violence before he had
reached his forties, his whereabouts at the time of other similar disappearances or known killings over the past twenty
years is still under investigation.

Out of the eleven murders he admitted, the bodies of
only four of his victims had been discovered before his final
arrest; all had been concealed in the vast tracts of cranberry
bogs and wooded areas where he had taken them in his
rented van. The fate of the others could be guessed, but
officially their names stood as those of missing persons.

What was the bait he set to catch so many in so short a
period? There was evidence that in many, possibly all, cases
the victims had drunk pop laced with rye and chloral hydrate
—the classic knockout drops, or Mickey Finn—before their
death, but that does not explain how they came to be
willingly in his company. The answer to that has to be that
this short, tough, wary-looking man, thief, burglar and in-
former was also a natural con-artist: glib, friendly, admiring,
nice mannered and supremely self-confident.

As a youth of eighteen, he had been judged "the most
sportsmanlike boxer" in a Golden Gloves tournament. When
he was serving time in the Saskatchewan Penitentiary in

Prince Albert in 1977, his bearing persuaded the Saskatchewan Criminal Compensation Board to make him an award of $3,500 for displaying an "unusual degree of moral and physical courage"; this arose out of seven stabbings he received from fellow-inmates after informing on two convicts planning to smuggle drugs into the penitentiary. He was, in short, a completely unprincipled charmer capable of performances able to win the trust of people far more sophisticated than teenagers.

Shrewd and cunning to a point. During his same term in Prince Albert in 1976, he had informed on another prisoner, Gary Marcoux, whom he had conned into boasting of the details of the slaying of a nine-year-old girl from Mission, B.C., whose body had been found tied to a tree in a remote forested area of the Fraser Valley. It was the evidence needed to bring Marcoux a life sentence, and it would be interesting to know what means Olson had used to make Marcoux imagine he could trust him with the knowledge. He was cunning enough to be able to escape police surveillance in 1981. Shrewd enough, even when convinced the police had enough evidence to put him away for life for at least one of the murders, to sense that they would nevertheless be willing to make some major concession in exchange for information that would not only solve so many mysterious disappearances, but put an end to the climate of terror he had created in the province.

Whether or not he was right in supposing that he was inevitably destined to receive a life sentence or even conviction without a confession is likely to remain a hypothetical question. Federal Solicitor General Robert Kaplan later maintained a solid case against Olson could have been made in respect of the four bodies already recovered. British Columbia's Attorney General Allan Williams said a deal was made only "to put to rest the uncertainty and grief" of the parents of the still missing children "and to give the victims a Christian burial."

But Inspector Proke of the RCMP was reported as saying

that "police believed they did not have enough evidence to support a single charge of first-degree murder," and John Hall, who was engaged to act as the Crown prosecutor, said that the evidence was "totally insufficient for a murder charge."

Whatever the truth and whatever the reasons, Olson was not only able to negotiate a deal that rocked the nation when it was disclosed in court five months later, but shrewd enough to have a lawyer draw up terms and conditions that were to make it impossible for the authorities to find an excuse to withhold payment if he fulfilled his part of the bargain.

In effect, this provided for the creation of a $100,000 trust fund in favor of Olson's wife and infant son, into which a lump sum of $30,000 would be paid when Olson gave further details in respect of the killings of the two boys and two girls whose bodies had already been discovered, and further amounts of $10,000 each for the same assistance in respect of the other seven killings, including discovery of the still missing bodies. There is evidence that the police may have originally intended to attempt to recover this money later, but he had circumvented them. By the time of the trial, only one amount of $10,000 remained unpaid, withheld on the grounds that one body had been beyond identification.

Regarded simply as an investment to safeguard the possibility of an acquittal, to provide reassurance to the public at large and at least the removal of uncertainty to the bereaved parents, to shorten the length of a trial once expected to take weeks and to avoid the heavy cost of continuous surveillance which would have to be incurred if Olson had received anything less than the maximum sentence, the payment can be abundantly justified. On the other hand, the deal was, at the least unusual, and probably unique in Canadian criminal history. Almost everybody would be initially shocked at the idea, many would find it morally repugnant and some would suggest it created a dangerous precedent. But, although the question was also raised, it was found that such a deal was in no way illegal under Canadian legislation.

Probably for these and other reasons—advance publicity would unquestionably make it difficult to empanel an unprejudiced jury if Olson entered a "not guilty" plea—the B. C. Attorney General Allan Williams requested local television and radio stations and the newspapers to withhold news of the deal before the trial, although the facts were known to their reporters. The news media met his request, but too many people knew of it for the deal to remain a well-kept secret in any Canadian city for long.

In consequence, the national media were prepared to give the matter the fullest play when the case came to trial; Olson's last-minute decision to enter a "guilty" plea added further drama to the occasion. His plea resulted in eleven concurrent life sentences which would normally carry eligibility for parole after twenty-five years, but Judge McKay stated he would recommend to the parole officials that Olson should never be freed.

News of the deal, made public for the first time, created the foreseen sensation and emotional outburst, intensified by the revelation that four of the killings had been done after the police had tried to keep Olson under surveillance as their chief suspect. For this to have occurred was obviously deplorable, but far from aggravating the distastefulness of the subsequent deal—which was how many people saw it—it seems to explain the necessity for it. The police were not only shorthanded but dealing with a seasoned, streetwise criminal adept at spotting and evading observation, experienced in covering his tracks.

But this was all taking place in a period in which the reputation of the mighty Royal Canadian Mounted Police—British Columbia being one of the eight Canadian provinces which have contracts with the RCMP for policing services—was at a low ebb. Now the once greatly respected service, already accused of an arrogant disregard of Canadian laws and constitutional procedures, was being portrayed as incompetent and immoral. Before the storm subsided, the Attorney General of British Columbia, the federal Solicitor General, the

Commissioner and Deputy Commissioner of the RCMP in Ottawa and finally the Prime Minister of Canada, were all drawn into the controversy.

The Olson case was a thoroughly nasty business from beginning to end. By body count, it was not the largest occurrence of mass-murder in Canada; that gruesome distinction goes to the destruction of all twenty-three passengers aboard a Dakota in 1949 by the Montreal jeweller Joseph Guay for the sole purpose of killing his wife. But Olson's crimes were more excruciating because of the months of horror and terror they caused. And they were certainly responsible for the most ominously mystifying series of disappearances in Canadian history.

RCMP officers in Vancouver have acknowledged that errors and misjudgements were made in the course of the investigation. This was undoubtedly so, although it must be recognized that apparently mindless murders committed singly and in isolation present exceptional problems with often agonizingly slow solutions. The Yorkshire Ripper killings in England, and those in Atlanta, Georgia, are famous examples although the bodies of the victims in both those cases were soon discovered. When bodies are concealed, the problems are greater.

By contrast, it can be noted that Olson's arrest in Vancouver came within nine months from the first of all the murders to which he confessed—within five months, in fact, of all but one. Not an epic performance . . . but better than that achieved in other jurisdictions.

Unusual Disturbance
in Forest Hill

Newspapers stand committed to tell the truth, although not always the whole truth, or even as much as reporters may know at the time their stories are written. Much of it is often irrelevant to the main story, some of it might prove actionable. Information that might serve as a danger signal to criminals may have to be temporarily withheld while the investigation of a serious crime is in progress.

So it was that when Frederick Johnsen made a dramatic departure from his home on Tuesday, August 28, 1979, all that the public at first learned was that a little before nine-thirty a wealthy forty-four-year-old businessman had been abducted at gunpoint in his wife's sight from their stately home at 93 Old Forest Hill Road, in the heart of Toronto's leafy Forest Hill area. It was a time of worldwide kidnapping with corporation executives and members of very rich families as favorite targets, and the bare facts at once conjured the image of a middle-aged man, educated, cultured and perhaps gone a little soft, held to ransom by underworld toughs.

This was somewhat at variance from the picture that began to emerge for reporters investigating the background, and during the day veiled hints in the press and on the air suggested that Frederick George Johnsen was a more colorful personality than the first image supposed. The following day, with a strong nudge from the police, who indicated that "further references to certain alleged business activities of Mr. Johnsen may hamper the police investigation," reporters were holding back some of the material coming to light.

Even so, the report of the manner of the abduction was in itself enough to arouse both wonder and surprise at the audacity of the kidnapper, for it was apparently a single-handed coup. Most abductions are carried out by a well-rehearsed team after long observation of the victim's usual habits, and in circumstances making it unlikely for the victim's disappearance to be discovered until enough time has passed for the abductors to leave a cold trail. Here, it seemed, the raider had relied on effrontery, surprise and panic.

The presence of three automobiles in the driveway must have alerted the uninvited visitor to the likely presence of witnesses, yet he had calmly come to the front door and rung the bell. The Johnsens kept no servants, so it was the blond, Danish-born Lisa Johnsen who went to open the door to the unimpressive figure on the porch clutching a parcel. "He was short, very fat and quite ugly," she told the police later. "He had a funny appearance, and looked like he could have been in his thirties or forties, with long, very black hair, which could have been a wig, under a little cap." If it was a wig it seems to have been his only attempt at disguise. Her first impression was that the caller looked a loser, one of life's underdogs.

Producing some documents out of the parcel, he told her they required her husband's signature. Lisa Johnsen offered to sign for them herself, but he insisted that it was Frederick Johnsen who had to sign them. Assuming then that the papers had something to do with the purchase of the house into which they had only recently moved, she turned to call her husband who was in the kitchen with her sister Evy and Evy's husband, Youcef Debabi. When the stranger had arrived, all four of them had been busy there unpacking belongings brought from the Johnsen's former home.

Fred Johnsen did not appear immediately, so his wife

called to him again, her back still to the front door. In the interval, the short, fat, ugly visitor had quietly eased his way into the hall uninvited and closed the door behind him. A few moments later, Johnsen appeared. When Lisa Johnsen turned, she realized that, from somewhere behind the parcel he had been carrying, her visitor was now leveling a small black gun at her husband.

What then ensued would likely have struck an uninvolved spectator more as a scene from farce than from crime melodrama. Fred Johnsen let out a yelp and started running, with his would-be abductor lumbering heavily in pursuit, in and out of the various rooms on the main floor, including the dining room and adjoining kitchen where Mr. and Mrs. Debabi could only gape at the spectacle in astonishment. For some reason, Johnsen kept screaming, "You've made a mistake! I'm not Fred Johnsen! You've got the wrong man!" while his pursuer puffed entreaties to him to slow down, nobody was going to hurt him.

Lisa Johnsen knew she must call the police, but the telephone in their new home had not yet been connected. With the chase still in progress, she teetered in her high heels across the lawn, out of the gateway and into the driveway of their neighbors to ring the bell and beg the use of their phone. It took only minutes, but they were valuable minutes for the abductor. Before the police had arrived, he had disappeared. So had Fred Johnsen.

How they had left was not known. Johnsen's own turbocharged Porsche, Lisa Johnsen's Rolls Royce and his brother-in-law's Jaguar sedan still stood in the driveway and in her dash for help, Lisa Johnsen had not observed a fourth car either in the drive or on the roadway—but that, of course, meant little since her mind was necessarily occupied with her husband's safety.

Later there would be mention of "a small foreign car" outside the house with possibly someone in the front seat, but it was too vague to constitute firm evidence. So far as anyone could tell, it had been a one-man snatch, and it could only be presumed that captor and captive, or possibly pursued and pursuer, had made their departure from the front of the house since everything had happened too fast for either Youcef or Evy Debabi to be clear just what had happened.

From a reading of the account, however, one thing at least seemed certain: Frederick Johnsen was a good catch for any ambitious kidnapper. The Forest Hill address and the luxury automobiles alone suggested wealth. The subsequent news that the mansion into which he, Lisa and their thirteen-year-old daughter Nicole were only just beginning to settle had cost $446,000—and that renovations included such niceties as gold-plated bathroom fixtures and a sauna were reputedly bringing the total to a figure closer to $600,000—reinforced the impression.

The Johnsens, it seemed, were indeed people of substance. Frederick Johnsen was president of British United Automobiles and of Downtown Fine Motors, and held a controlling interest in three companies in the electronic industry. Together, the Johnsens were the owners of several nursing homes and, before moving into Forest Hill, had owned a substantial private residence in Mississauga, a rich but newer community to the west of the city, without quite the same social distinction that the Forest Hill address enjoyed. A vulnerable target, indeed.

However, after two days had passed without the arrival of any message or demand, it began to look as if this might not have been an ordinary kidnap-for-ransom at all. What was the alternative? Minds turned automatically to the disappearance of Jimmy Hoffa, the former boss of the Teamsters' Union, who vanished in Detroit in 1975 in a no less mysterious and ominous way. Hoffa undoubtedly had enemies and rivals. Might the same be true of Frederick Johnsen?

His business associates scoffed at the idea. "He's a very decent citizen, popular with everybody," said one. "Who can't like the guy?" Another insisted that although Johnsen was an extremely gifted wheeler-dealer, "all the deals he was involved in were aboveboard." A third spoke angrily of "the dirty pack of lies and the rumors that have come about why he was kidnapped."

Through Johnsen's lawyer, they issued the telephone number for a continuously manned "command post" they had organized to receive communications from or about the kidnappers, and emphasized that confidentiality would be preserved. The police in turn provided a stiff-sounding comment to the effect that the lawyer was a private citizen and could do what he wanted, "even if it impeded the police investigation." The private line was deluged with calls but apparently, apart from the inevitable bogus demands, prank calls and curiosity seekers, none threw light on Fred Johnsen's fate or his whereabouts.

One bogus ransom demand specified a location on River Street where money was to be left at a certain time. A dummy bundle was duly deposited and kept under observation from a concealed point but it was left untouched. A confusingly worded ransom demand, illiterately written, was discovered in the washrooms in the Simpson's store in the Yorkdale Mall—it was impossible to tell whether the amount specified was sixty thousand or a million dollars—and, although it was almost certainly a hoax, a coded message was placed in the Toronto *Star* as the writer had instructed. Again, just as expected, it drew no reply.

A few mornings later the employees arriving at one of Johnsen's automobile showrooms found that another joker had sprayed the words "Fred's dead" across the plate-glass window sometime during the night. Like all the other responses that the publicity had generated, it gave no indication of being the work of the kind of professional crook expected to be responsible for Fred Johnsen's disappearance.

To this point, Johnsen's business associates had not been publicly identified; all that had been stated was that their authorized spokesman, Johnsen's own lawyer, Ted Horton, was a member of the eminent civil law firm of Fraser and Beatty. Presumably they began wondering whether one major reason they had heard nothing from the underworld was simply a matter of distrust; Ted Horton so clearly belonged to the other world of law-abiding civil litigation, leases and contracts that he lacked credibility as a confidential negotiator with those familiar only with the criminal courts. In effect, he and they spoke in different languages.

This would explain why after three days Johnsen's associates decided to dismantle the "command post" and Ted Horton arranged for the celebrated criminal lawyer, David Humphrey, to make himself available as a more approachable intermediary. David Humphrey in turn called a press conference at the Johnsen home on Sunday, September 2, when he stated that his role was "in no way connected with the police investigation," and confirmed that he spoke on behalf of businessmen "who collectively have access to an amount of money necessary to negotiate Mr. Johnsen's release."

Two of them, Jack Witte, a partner in British United Automobiles, and Andre Rivera of New Jersey were present; asked later how many others were part of the group he represented, Ted Horton would not be specific, but said all except Andre Rivera were from the Toronto area. Andre Rivera, a Dominican national, had flown up from New Jersey immediately upon learning of Fred Johnsen's disappearance; he was, it was to prove, one of the missing man's oldest business friends, and their business relationship had increased greatly over the years.

The press conference brought prompt results—of a sort. A man phoned David Humphrey the day after a report of the conference had appeared, claiming to know where Johnsen was being held, and indicating that his knowledge had a price. From his experience, Humphrey sensed that this was at least not an amateur prankster, but a man who knew his way around the back streets. He reported the conversation to Andre Rivera, who had remained in Toronto staying at the elegant Park Plaza Hotel. When Humphrey's caller rang back, a meeting was set up for him to talk to Rivera at the considerably less elegant Roehampton Place Hotel on Mount Pleasant Road, at which lawyers on both sides would be present. But the meeting could not be described as a success.

As David Humphrey had known, his caller—now identified as Howard "Mugsy" Dean—was indeed a member of the Toronto underworld in good standing, with a record of convictions including theft, forgery, breaking and entry and acquittal on a charge of murder, going back to the time when he was nineteen, twenty-five years earlier. He did not claim responsibility for the abduction, only to know Johnsen's whereabouts and the reason he was being held. Johnsen, he said, owed certain parties a matter of $28,000 and the amount now owing to cover this, and include collection expenses to date, was $53,000. He offered his services to secure the captive's release, and indicated his certainty that Johnsen would "remain disappeared" until the account was paid in full.

It should be stated here that, as all his associates knew and many reporters had learned, Fred Johnsen's ceaseless buyings, sellings and tradings frequently caused him cash-flow problems, with the consequence that it was true enough that he might have some impatient creditors at any time. It was also a fact that in recent years he had discovered the excitement of green baize gambling tables. Only the previous day, in fact, when Lisa Johnsen had been asked by a *Globe and Mail* reporter whether her husband might be described as a gambler, she had given the equivocal answer, "Not really, at least, never in Toronto. He did enjoy going to Las Vegas two or three times a year." Las Vegas operators are not generally ranked among the most patient creditors.

On the one hand, therefore, Dean's story had a degree of credibility. On the other, those facts about Johnsen's life-style would be far from inaccessible to anyone with Dean's worldly experience. Furthermore, he could supply none of the kind of authentification David Humphrey had suggested at the press conference: a photograph, verifiable as recently taken, or some identifiable possessions carried by the missing man. Andre Rivera was far from being fully convinced, but reluctant to abruptly discard the only potentially valid response they had elicited. He accordingly gave Dean $1,000 which he said was all he carried with him, and told him the balance would only be paid on Johnsen's safe return.

There may have been some discussion about a further meeting (subsequent evidence was not clear on this point), but what seems to have happened is that a review of the meeting with Johnsen's other associates convinced Andre Rivera that his initial doubts of Dean's credibility were confirmed by what had been learned of his previous record. The promise of confidentiality for any bona fide negotiator given at the press conference obviously no longer applied. The approach Dean had made and the amount he had specified as being required for Johnsen's release were accordingly revealed to the police, and on September 7, only five days after the press conference, Howard Daniel "Mugsy" Dean was arrested by Metro police and charged with extortion.

And then on September 27, less than three weeks later and as a result of a remarkable coincidence, a short, fat, ugly man identified as Allen (Allan, or Alan—accounts differ) Eugene Bazkur, also known as Allen Bass, aged thirty-eight, was arrested at his breakfast in the Tivoli restaurant on Yonge Street on a charge of kidnapping Frederick George Johnsen.

Neither man was allowed bail. Dean's trial on the charge of extortion began in February 1980. A preliminary inquiry into the kidnapping, arising out of Bazkur's arrest, was held in January, but his trial did not take place until May of that year. Until then, the public had learned little of the case against either man. They had, however, come to hear a good deal more about the missing man, things which now seemed might have some relevance to his disappearance.

The imagined picture of Frederick Johnsen as an educated man of gentle birth had soon dissolved with the knowledge that he was an orphan from New Brunswick who had been adopted there as a child by a Scandinavian potato-farming family, and had never finished high school. He had lived

with the family near Grand Falls, taking his part in working
the land until his early twenties, and had then made his way
to Toronto in 1958. Four years later he had married Lisa, an
emigrant from Denmark, and started his first business.

It was a store dealing in reconditioned electrical ap-
pliances and television sets, mostly bargain-sale trade-ins from
U.S. hotels and motels purchased from the same Andre Rivera
of New Jersey, who was to become his associate and partner
in other more ambitious projects over the next seventeen
years. The store had prospered, and by 1970 Fred and Lisa
had established themselves comfortably in King City, some
ten miles to the north of Toronto. For some reason they decided to put some of their profits into purchasing a part-in-
terest in a nursing home located in that quiet, pleasant town;
a sound investment in an age in which the elderly form a
larger proportion of the population every year, but not one
that might be imagined as the first choice of an ambitious
young couple in their early thirties.

Possibly Fred was making a lucky guess, possibly he was
showing a glimpse of his nose for a bargain, or possibly his
sharp ears had caught a rumor. Whatever the inspiration, the
investment was amply rewarded when, only two years later,
the Ontario Government announced that the Ontario Health
Insurance Plan would be extended to include nursing home
care. That year, nursing homes started to become the hottest
investment tip across the province. No new home could be
operated without a license, and henceforward nobody with a
licensed home need want for patients.

With two years of experience in the nursing-home business and the talent for bargaining and trading he had developed in the used appliance business behind him, Fred Johnsen was not only in on the ground floor of a burgeoning
industry but much better equipped than most investors. He
and Lisa at once bought out their partners in King City
Lodge and set about acquiring other nursing homes in other
cities.

It was not his style to establish a large or enduring chain;

rather, he bought units for prices he saw as advantageous and sold them again as soon as he had made them more profitable or when the investment climate had made them more valuable. In an extremely thoroughly researched story appearing in the Toronto *Globe and Mail* on September 20, 1979, Peter Moon listed the nursing homes Johnsen had bought and sold up to 1978; they included establishments in King City, Toronto, Wiarton, St. Williams, St. Thomas and Southampton. By July 1978 he still owned another nursing home in Toronto and had extended his holdings outside Ontario to include a partnership with his old friend Andre Rivera in nursing home operations in California, Texas and Florida.

Moon also traced Johnsen's incursion into the retail automobile business to his purchase of a car dealership, SCU Industries Ltd., when it was in receivership in 1976. From this beginning, British United Automobiles, Downtown Fine Cars, Coventry Motors Ltd. and Vintage Grand Touring Automobiles, together with ownership of some much prized real estate had all developed. Later had come Komar Investments, a holding company for three others making electronic components and circuit boards, a G.M. dealership in Texas and a half-interest shared with his brother-in-law Youcef Debabi in a company called the Home Juice Corporation.

His holdings were in a constant state of flux with deals often arranged to sell all or part of a new purchase before it had been concluded, so his disappearance inevitably introduced huge problems and vast confusion. The more so because many of his deals existed only as handshake agreements, and as earlier noted, he tended to use money due to his creditors to finance new deals for as long as possible. Moon illustrated this propensity by citing the evidence he gave under examination in a suit taken against him by real estate brokers in July 1978 for payment of $21,000 commission still owing on the sale of the Southampton Nursing Home four months earlier.

The transcript shows Johnsen as a master of parrying questions relating to his income and cash resources with answers that somehow succeeded in creating more obscurity than previously existed. Asked whether there was a possibility of getting money together from other sources to pay the amount owing, he answered, "Possibly there would be." Invited to enlarge on that possibility, he explained, "Well, if I decide I am going to pay it, then I guess I will pay it." To the inquiry whether this meant he could pay it without difficulty, he allowed, "I probably could, yes." In this case, he finally agreed to pay the money over the next six months.

Three days after the date of Johnsen's disappearance, Moon discovered, he would have to have come up with $3,050,000 to complete the purchase of two nursing homes, one in Newmarket and the other in Bradford, for which he had paid a deposit of $25,000 in August 1977; the deal had been held up since that date by a dispute over mortgaging, but differences had recently been resolved. In the meantime—in fact, less than a month after he had paid his deposit—Johnsen had resold the Newmarket nursing home for a profit of more than a quarter of a million and had taken a $10,000 deposit.

Now, with his companies unable to pay the three million odd dollars on the due date, the deal fell through. Johnsen had lost his $25,000 deposit, and the prospective purchaser of the Newmarket home not only lost what would have been a profitable investment (a freeze on nursing home licenses had by 1979 greatly increased the going price for the Newmarket home), but was out close to $14,000 paid in land transfer taxes, and faced the problem of recovering the deposit of $10,000.

This was typical of the financial chaos caused by Johnsen's absence. Later it would be found that another of his companies had contracted to pay the City of Toronto approximately $1,575,000 by March 1, 1980, as the major payment of a ninety-nine-year lease on land on which a combination of a nursing home and an apartment building was to be built. Construction was in progress when he disappeared, but was soon halted. When the deadline for the payment came, the company would be unable to meet it; the value of the work already done was virtually absorbed by mechanics' liens placed by unpaid sub-contractors.

In his profile of the life and times of Frederick Johnsen, Peter Moon also spoke of his love of gambling in which baccarat had recently replaced craps as his passion, and found a delicate way to refer to another side of Johnsen's personality of which little had previously been spoken publicly.

"His loyalty to old friends and his gambling," he wrote, "meant that Mr. Johnsen had many friends who sometimes seemed incongruous for a rising millionaire businessman." One friend in particular, he mentioned, was Walter Chomski who had served two jail terms for bookmaking offenses, and who had lost his right leg in December 1974 when, by lowering his weight into the driver's seat of his Lincoln Continental, he set off the booby trap someone had arranged for him during the night. Perhaps Walter Chomski had some idea who that somebody might have been, but no arrest was made; now, however, he was generally accompanied by an attacktrained Doberman pinscher when he took the air.

How, or in what circumstances, Walter Chomski had met Frederick Johnsen was not explained. That they were close friends there was no doubt; once a week at least Chomski dropped in on Johnsen at Downtown Fine Cars to shoot the breeze. Nothing could be amiss, of course, with Fred Johnsen choosing whatever friends he wished, and both men shared an interest in gambling, though on opposite sides of the fence. For those who were starting to think that Johnsen's disappearance was not to be explained as an abduction for ransom, however, it provided evidence that the missing man was at least not unfamiliar with a world in which a man might meet a sudden, violent end at unfriendly hands.

This is an account of a disappearance, not of the two prosecutions resulting from it. There were, however, bizarre features of each to match the freakish nature of the whole case. At the trial of Howard "Mugsy" Dean on the charge of extorting $1,000, the evidence given by Andre Rivera was confirmed not only by Ted Horton but by Dean's own lawyer at that time, Kenneth Danson, and Danson's partner, Symon Zucker.

Dean, it appears, had outsmarted himself by arranging for their attendance. His idea seems to have been to secure respectable witnesses who could testify that he had disavowed responsibility for the kidnap, and had simply offered his services as an uninvolved intermediary on the basis of his familiarity with the underworld. But he had, of course, gone considerably beyond that by claiming knowledge of Johnsen's whereabouts, the reason for the kidnap, the payoff demanded and the consequences of its non-payment, and Danson and Zucker could only confirm those facts.

In these circumstances, Dean was not unexpectedly represented in court by a new lawyer, Joseph Bloomenfeld, who did his best to argue that the $1,000 his client took from Rivera was understood as being only to cover actual expenses and that Dean had no designs on any part of the other $50,000 odd discussed. However, neither the evidence as to what had actually been said at the meeting, nor Dean's behavior in court—he had already accused Rivera, Horton, Danson and Zucker of a conspiracy of perjury, and was later to discharge his new lawyer—persuaded the jury to see him as the altruist he claimed to be, only seeking to do a favor to a family he did not know.

He had also accused the police of implying that he had suggested the names of those he believed responsible for the abduction—which he strenuously denied doing—for the purpose of setting him up for a hit. And, sure enough, on the eve of the jury's verdict, a telephone call was indeed made to Bloomenfeld's law office to the effect that he and Dean would be killed at the courthouse on the following day. That information was duly relayed to Judge Ferguson, who immediately ordered special precautionary measures to be taken, and Dean granted permission to the press to report the event. The threats were made by "people very capable of carrying them out," he told them. The incident caused a sensation, but no attempt was made, and there is no way of knowing who made the telephone call.

Ten weeks later, Allan Bazkur stood trial in another court on the charge of kidnapping Frederick Johnsen. At the pre- liminary hearing in January, Bazkur had proved to be a Polish-Irish ex-boxer, five foot seven in height and some 200 pounds in weight, looking, with black hair combed across a balding head, rather older than his thirty-eight years. He had also proved to be a man with a stormy relationship with a for- mer beauty contestant of the same age, Sandra Cohen.

It has been mentioned that Bazkur had come to the police's attention as a consequence of an odd coincidence. It had happened in this way. Shortly before Johnsen's disap- pearance, Sandra Cohen had informed Bazkur that she had performed fellatio for a police officer to avoid being ticketed for a minor driving offense at a time when her driving license had been suspended. Bazkur, seeing the incident as providing a claim for large compensation, had launched a campaign against provincial and municipal authorities. As a conse- quence, a police officer attached to the Peel Regional force had resigned, but that fell considerably short of the restitu- tion Bazkur was seeking. He continued campaigning forcibly enough to make his presence familiar to numerous Metro officers—one of whom suddenly entertained the possibility that this somewhat overweight man of less-than-average- height, fortyish and considerably less than handsome, with a minor record of convictions, might just be the short, fat, ugly hood of thirty or forty Lisa Johnsen had described.

The police had fifteen other active suspects at the time, but Bazkur's resemblance to the description, his criminal con- nections and his way of life—most of his time was spent in Times Square Billiards, and welfare payments of some $200 a month had constituted his only known means of support for the past year—amply justified his addition to the list. He did not have the appearance of a man able to live comfortably on less than fifty dollars a week, and although he first told the police that he had spent the evening of August 28 in the bil-

liards hall on Edward Street, nobody else seemed to remember it.

The investigation proceeded, now with a little help from
Sandra Cohen, who about this time had undergone one of the
violent arguments with Bazkur that had periodically charac-
terized their seven-year relationship. (It was presumably the
healing of this latest breach that subsequently made her such
a reluctant witness.) The evidence against Bazkur was becoming stronger, but was not as conclusive as the police
would have liked. For instance, his was one of the two photographs out of a big pile handed her for inspection to be
picked by Evy Debabi, and after further thought, she had settled for Bazkur as the intruder on the night of August 28. But
she had only declared herself "90 percent certain." And Lisa
Johnsen, after looking through some five hundred photographs, had been unable to make a selection.

Lisa Johnsen attended two lineups, the first of which included other key suspects, while the second included Bazkur.
At the first, she tentatively identified a man of somewhat similar appearance, but said she was not sure. At the second, she
identified Bazkur immediately, saying, "It's number eight. It's
him. My God, it's him." She became violently agitated, and
had to be helped from the room. On the other hand, it
transpired later that since the lineup had been hastily arranged, none of the others, who were volunteers, bore much
resemblance to the man she had described.

But there was also the matter of the watch; shortly after
Johnsen's disappearance, Bazkur was known to have tried to
sell a slim gold watch of the same make as the missing man's
to a shopkeeper. With all that and Bazkur's continued inability to provide an alibi for the evening of August 28, it was
enough for an arrest.

At the preliminary hearing in January, however, the evidence about the gold watch lost its venom when the defense
was able to produce the alleged watch in question, found in a
duffel bag in a friend's room, and it was shown to be of
14-karat gold, and not the purer 18-karat gold watch that

Johnsen sported. Sandra Cohen was an uncooperative witness, too. But, probably largely because of Lisa Johnsen's positive identification, a sufficiently strong prima facie case was established for Bazkur to stand trial in May.

When that time came, Lisa Johnsen was the first witness called and was positive in her identification. ("That's the man, right there . . . Mr. Bazkur.") And later in the trial, the prosecution was able to put a seventeen-year-old youth in the box who testified that as one of Bazkur's fellow-inmates of the Don Jail, he had spoken with him and heard him claim to be responsible for Johnsen's disappearance. Damaging evidence to read, but there was no corroboration of the conversation, and it can be assumed that the youth's unsupported evidence was not entirely convincing: asked to comment on it by his own lawyer, William Parker, Bazkur said flatly, "I have never seen him in my entire life. I never had a conversation with that gentleman in my entire life." Not too many points for the prosecution on that round, it seems.

But for the prosecution worse was to come when it appeared that Bazkur was now quite prepared to agree that he had not been, as he had at first stated, in Times Square Billiards on the evening of August 28. Not only had he since remembered that he had spent the evening in the bar of the Hampton Court Hotel on Jarvis Street, but could prove it. His old friend, the barman there, remembered it because, ironically enough, he had been paying for his drinks with somebody else's Chargex card which he had "found in a park" about two weeks earlier. There was a copy of the Chargex slip, and a handwriting expert to give his opinion that the signature "G. W. Watson" was in the writing of Allan Bazkur, and there was the CBC journalist he had been buying drinks for, and who remembered a singularly pointless conversation they had exchanged about the peanuts that the bar no longer provided, and recalled the large bag of cashews toted that evening by the lady who was their drinking companion.

The journalist and the barman indeed confirmed the evidence, the barman admitting that he had earlier denied it because he thought the police were investigating the misuse of credit cards, and had no wish to expose his own indiscretion.

After that bombshell, the case against Allan Bazkur virtually collapsed, with his acquittal assured.

The verdict was a triumph for Bazkur's lawyer, William Parker, and a bitter defeat for the Crown. There had been other key suspects, but the positive identification Lisa Johnsen had made of Bazkur in effect offered them immunity. From the day after the "not guilty" verdict was delivered, a sense of anti-climax was felt. For most of the media, Fred Johnsen became the forgotten man. A short newspaper item the next month reported that his description had been supplied to the county coroner in Buffalo, New York, to see if it in any way matched a badly decomposed body taken ashore three miles from the mouth of the Niagara River; it did not, but nobody had really expected otherwise. There, it seemed, matters would rest.

Oddly enough, though, an alternative theory did exist. It had been loudly and frequently proclaimed by "Mugsy" Dean and had formed part of lawyer William Parker's case for Bazkur's defense, although it received little attention from the media at the time. It did not receive justice until, on the first anniversary of Fred Johnsen's disappearance, Barbara Amiel, then a senior writer for *Maclean's* magazine wrote a cover story, "Where Is Fred Johnsen?" (*Maclean's*, August 25, 1980) that took the official lid off the untold story. She was able to reveal what had gone on at Bazkur's preliminary hearing (a ban on publication of evidence had applied at the time), provided thumbnail sketches of all the principals—and grimy thumbnails they were, too—set out certain previously unpublicized incidents relating to Fred Johnsen's early days in Toronto, and aired what could be called the street theory of what had really happened. It was scintillating journalism and some of the facts already given have, with the permission of Barbara Amiel and *Maclean's*, been derived from it.

By the time it appeared, she could also disclose that in 1959, the year after his arrival in Toronto, Johnsen had been taken to serve a three-month sentence in the Mimico Correctional Centre on a breaking-and-entering conviction, and that in the following year two counts of "theft over $50" had drawn him eighteen months at the Burwash Correctional Centre.

It has been stated elsewhere that in his early Toronto years he had employment as a stationery engineer; even if this was so, one of the minor mysteries of the case has been how the young farm laborer from New Brunswick found the capital to open a used appliance store within four years of arrival, and form his profitable association with Andre Rivera in New Jersey. That was answered in an enlightening interview Amiel had with Johnsen's old friend, Walter Chomski, the bookmaker-moneylender who lost a leg when his Lincoln Continental exploded.

It was Chomski, it proved, who had advanced some of the money that allowed Johnsen to open up a business. He had, he told Amiel, spotted him early on as a potential high-roller, and they had soon become close personal friends, delighting in each other's company. When the attempt on Chomski's life had landed him in St. John's Convalescent Hospital in North York, Johnsen had visited him and played cards almost daily. "I loved him," Chomski said simply. "He was an amoral charming con man."

They holidayed together, partied together, went on gambling sprees together, sometimes on the spur of the moment. "If Fred had stayed in the nursing home business he would have been the multimillionaire he thought he was," Chomski reflected. "But he didn't want to be just a nursing home proprietor. He had this Howard Hughes idea that he'd be a tycoon with all sorts of business interests." Other interests, too, apparently. As another of Johnsen's close associates murmured, "He could never, but never, turn down the ladies."

Which leads to the street theory of Fred Johnsen's disappearance: it was a dramatic presentation conceived, produced and orchestrated by Fred himself. The arguments in favor of the theory carry some weight. His companies collectively were committed to the bank for something like $7 million, and it seemed uncertain whether the total was matched by assets, some of the companies were losing money, and besides company debts he had personal loans of $145,000 outstanding, and even after months of investigation, police auditors were still coming on fresh tangles to unravel. The reasons for making a disappearance at that time might have been overwhelming.

Consider, then, the circumstances of the disappearance. An abduction in front of witnesses, able to raise a prompt alarm and describe the abductor. A single abductor, too, for God's sake, of no impressive size or agility. Who would plan such a brazen caper? Only someone wanting to make it appear that the disappearance was involuntary and under duress; someone who *wanted* the incident to be witnessed.

"He wanted the prestige of the big-car showrooms, the windows with the Corniches in them. Prestige!" Walter Chomski told Barbara Amiel. "It all got out of hand for him. He's probably in Mexico or Brazil now." "Mugsy" Dean had said much the same thing: "He's laying in the sun with some nice young chick spending the money that he conned people out of." "Even if he did arrange his own kidnapping, he's never really hurt anyone. Not anyone that couldn't afford the loss," said one of his business acquaintances.

But to what extent were these the thoughts of the people who preferred not to think that ill could have befallen Fred Johnsen? The reasons for supposing Johnsen to be the victim of criminal vengeance are in their way just as persuasive. Everyone who knew Johnsen seems to have agreed that money, in terms of a fortune to be spent at leisure, meant nothing to him. "There were three things Freddy loved," one associate had told Peter Moon of the *Globe and Mail.* "He loved raising money and doing deals, he loved cars and he loved gambling." Would an eternity of "laying in the sun with some nice young chick" offer any strong temptation to such a personality? Could he refrain for long from the world's major gambling centers and from the kind of hectic wheeling and dealing that would eventually be certain to bring him under official scrutiny?

If he had engineered his own disappearance, it must have taken some advance planning. In which case, why had he only recently completed the purchase of the Forest Hill mansion and ordered such elaborate renovations? (Surely not as a farewell present for his wife; it was larger than she would need or be able to maintain. There was an outstanding balance of $387,000 on the mortgage alone, apart from the cost of the renovations.) Why would he have not delayed his departure for the few days required to turn a quick profit on the nursing homes in Newmarket and Bradford that he would have been able to acquire at bargain prices on August 31?

And one other major question: Who had been his accomplice, and by what means had Johnsen made certain of the accomplice's silence in view of the possibility of the offer of a large reward? Or the even greater possibility of the accomplice's arrest? Far more likely, surely, that the appearance of the intruder that evening was deliberate evidence of the retribution awaiting transgressors.

When Walter Chomski's Lincoln exploded, nobody thought it might have been an accident. Such an open act of malicious violence was doubtless intended to convey a message to others besides the victim. If there were others, too, who might learn a message from the fate befalling Fred Johnsen, is it not likely that, instead of an ambiguous disappearance in unknown circumstances, his enemies would plan his capture to be made in the presence of witnesses? The abduction could have been performed by an imported heavy who could be far from the scene within hours, leaving unseen killers to complete the contract and dispose of the body.

Peter Moon accepts the theory privately favored by most policemen, that Freddy Johnsen is dead. Johnsen's friends believe he is alive and well outside Canada. Based only on what is so far known, there remain puzzling features to either explanation. At this point it can only be said that whoever planned the unusual disturbance in Forest Hill that August evening seems to have succeeded.

A Summer Affair

To someone with a little money saved, and who is twenty, personable and unattached, being temporarily unemployed simply means having a good excuse to discover what excitements the world has to offer. Particularly when summer is near, and a powerful motorcycle stands ready. Since the long Victoria Day weekend of 1974 was coming up, Terry Turnbull decided to drive the 200 miles south from Copper Cliff, just outside Sudbury, to join the young crowds at Wasaga Beach.

Within hours he met the girl who, in the next five months, was to provide him with considerably more excitement and adventure than he had probably hoped to find. Lisa Golding (really Eleanor Joan Golding, but only her family back home now called her Eleanor) was tall and beautiful, with long, straight hair falling to her high, slim waist, and mischievous, knowing eyes. She was two years older than Terry, and like him was a keen biker. She had been touring around most of May on her new Kawasaki; as she told him, she had just been spending a couple of days in Hull, Quebec, with a girl who had been a close friend back in Nova Scotia. Lisa had ridden from Hull to Wasaga Beach to meet her new friends, Bill and Nancy Evans. They were her next-door neighbors in the Peterborough apartment building she had been living in since March, just two months ago, she explained. He must meet the Evanses, he'd like them.

Terry did. Terry liked everything about Lisa: her friends, her looks, her casual attire—she was one of the few girls who really looked neat in jeans, he decided—her frank speech and her animation. Soon she started talking again of the friend she had been holidaying with in Hull, whom she had not seen since she had left Halifax. In those days, she said, her friend had still been married. In fact, they both had. Well, as a matter of fact, she herself still was, kinda. But it just wasn't working out. She'd left Peterborough for a while to get her head straight, to decide what she had to do. (According to a statement given later by the friend in question, "Lisa came for two days. She was really messed up. She didn't know whether she was coming or going, or anything. She was tired of being married, and she just wanted to be single again.")

Lisa basked in Terry's interest and attention. When Bill Evans suggested Terry might look them up if he ever came to Peterborough, she insisted they should make a firm date for a reunion next week. He would be the Evans's houseguest.

Nevertheless, when the time came, the party given for him on the evening of his arrival was in the Golding apartment. Bill and Nancy Evans were there, so were two of their other friends, Bob and Linda Morrison—and so was Lisa's husband, Dennis.

It may have been an awkward moment for Terry Turnbull (which, incidentally, is the one name that has been changed in this account), but Dennis, near his twenty-fourth birthday, was an emotionally guarded and successful young real estate salesman who apparently gave no indication of recognizing anything unusual about the situation. Interestingly enough, it seems these two very different men formed something of a liking—possibly even an unconscious mutual sympathy—for each other. Certainly it was natural enough that Lisa and Terry, the two bike enthusiasts, should agree to ride out together the next morning to the Mosport track thirty miles away, just north of Oshawa. In return, Terry suggested

they should all come up to visit him in Sudbury during the
next week.

Little information is available about what Lisa and Terry
discussed during their day at Mosport. Terry summarized it
later as, "She told me things in general weren't going too
good, and she wanted to do something about it." From other
recollections he provided of subsequent conversations, it can
be gathered that Lisa indulged in a measure of exaggeration
and possibly fantasy to improve a story, so what she told
Terry can only be guessed. The bare facts, however, were
these.

Lisa's father had died when she and her elder brother
were quite young; she quarreled with her mother frequently
but had a good relationship with her step-father. Her brother
enlisted in the navy, and she herself left home soon after she
had graduated from high school and, after a mysterious but
brief fling in New York, took a job at a local bank. One weekend, at her parents' home, she had met Dennis Golding, then
also in the navy and her brother's closest friend. At that time
Lisa was seventeen.

Dennis's parents were divorced. His father lived in California, and his mother, who was born in the Netherlands, was
now married to a successful Dutch real estate broker in Peterborough. Lisa and Dennis began going out together when he
had leave. She soon gave up her job at the bank and started
work at a combined hamburger and fish-and-chip joint in
Halifax. Dennis, after living with her for a few months, then
married her in some style in All Saints Cathedral in the city.
His father came from California for the wedding, which was
also attended by his mother and his step-father from Peterborough, who took an immediate liking to his young step-son
and his beautiful bride.

With Dennis away at sea much of the time, Lisa's early
married life, living in Dartmouth with friends to visit and no
need to work, may have been the most carefree period she
had known. Even then, however, she had voiced her dissat-
isfaction with her new life to her neighbor, the same girl she

would later be seeing in Hull. Dennis, it appears, thought Lisa was improvident; he would willingly buy her anything she needed, but was reluctant to give her spending money. A good deal of the romance had also gone out of their lives; when Lisa and Dennis went dancing with the friend and her husband, Lisa and the husband were partners all the evening, as were Dennis and the friend. Both marriages were becoming rocky at the same time.

From Lisa's point of view, things became still more intolerable after Dennis left the service. He had already bought a local campground, and now all his time was taken up by starting a business career. He built a house, and although he sold it at a profit, it had the effect of turning his mind in the direction of the greater business opportunities he might find in Ontario, and of his step-father's successful realty operation in Peterborough. His step-father warmly applauded the idea. As a start, Dennis should take a real estate course. Then Dennis should join his business. And, his mother added, Dennis and Lisa should come and live with them.

Lisa objected violently. It would mean leaving her hometown and all the people she knew, and her family. Her young half-brother, to whom she was devoted, was ill, and would miss her. They knew nobody in Ontario, and the thought of living the life of a dutiful daughter-in-law in the home of strangers sickened her. She couldn't stand being fenced in. Dennis was determined to make the move. He wasn't a Maritimer; he had been born in Toronto, and his early years had been spent with his own father in the States. But he would compromise. They would take an apartment of their own, and he would buy Lisa a 350 Yamaha for Christmas; Lisa would be free to come and go as she pleased. So she had agreed to give it a chance.

Thus, after little more than two years of marriage, they had arrived in Peterborough in March 1974. Two months and one motorcycle later (it is difficult to discover why the Yamaha had to be replaced with the Kawasaki), Lisa had taken off "to get her head together." And now here she was, off for the day at Mosport with Terry, the sun shining and the wind in their hair.

The following weekend, true to their word, they all came up to Sudbury; Bill and Nancy, Bob and Linda, and Lisa. All, that is, but Dennis. And when they returned to Peterborough, Lisa told Dennis that Terry had mentioned he was taking a trip by himself to the east coast, and that she wanted to go along, just for the company. If Dennis wanted her to stay married to him, he had to trust her and allow her the freedom he had promised. She wanted to see her family again, and with Terry she would feel safe on the road. He was just a kid, for God's sake.

Dennis yielded unhappily, but he gave her some money for the road, the loan of his Chargex card and promised to phone her step-father in Halifax to confirm his approval of Terry as Lisa's escort. A few days later, Lisa and Terry were on their way. It was now the middle of June.

Terry was to say later that when Lisa had proposed accompanying him on the trip, he had wondered whether "it was a very good idea, because of Dennis." At twenty, however, one does not question opportunity and adventure too closely; in any case, the roller coaster was already moving, and he was aboard.

In Halifax, Lisa's mother and step-father, given her assurance that Terry "was a very good friend of Dennis's, and no hanky-panky was going on," decided Terry "seemed like a nice guy" and gave them a warm welcome. (Remarkably, with young and old alike, he apparently always created a favorable impression from the outset.) But even before they had reached Halifax, there must have been some barbed and spiky phone conversations with Peterborough. The question of a legal separation had been discussed, and Lisa had consulted a lawyer in Halifax on the subject while she was staying with her parents. Nevertheless, although the document was already prepared when she and Terry returned after an absence of three weeks, she went back to the Peterborough apartment, and Terry continued to Sudbury alone.

It seems fair to assume that by this point Lisa had reduced both Terry and Dennis to her own state of mental confusion. The separation papers were signed, and a few days later Lisa set out to join Terry in Sudbury. But a week later, she was back, alone, in Peterborough. Dennis asked her to leave, and she returned to Sudbury where she convinced Terry he should settle up his affairs and come with her to find a new life in western Canada. Ten days later, at the beginning of August, they started out with their few possessions on their motorcycles.

Postcards and phone calls from Manitoba, Saskatchewan, Alberta and British Columbia to her family and friends provided a record of their strange odyssey in search of a place to live and somewhere they could find work. A further sequence in fast-reverse indicated how unsuccessful it had proved, and how rapidly they decided each city had nothing to offer them. By the end of the month, they were back in Sudbury. But Sudbury was not what Lisa wanted, so in September they headed east to Halifax again. They continued to draw blanks, and by now funds were running low. So Lisa sent Terry back to Sudbury, and phoned Dennis in Peterborough to ask him for her air fare to Ontario to allow her to stay with her old girl friend (the one she had known in Halifax and had seen earlier in the year in Hull), who was living in Ajax, between Toronto and Oshawa.

Dennis did so. He apparently thought the request indicated that Lisa's little fling was over now that summer was ending. He made frequent calls from Peterborough to Ajax, to attempt a reconciliation. And Lisa made as many calls to Terry in Sudbury to tell him how much she was missing him. The lure was irresistible; before long, he was down in Ajax, had traded in his motorcycle on a car, and was ready to take up the search for the new life again. This time it would be in Ontario.

About this time, mid-September, it appears, not altogether surprisingly, that Dennis was speaking suicidally.
Whether he actually made an attempt at that time, as he said
he did, or whether he had only indicated a suicidal intention
to Lisa, is not clear. Possibly it was enough to halt her search;
this had been even briefer than the earlier attempts, being
confined to the towns between Hamilton and London. By
now, anyway, their funds were almost completely spent, and
she phoned her step-father in Halifax to see if he would help
them. He heard the story in dismay. The best thing for Lisa
to do, he said, was to fly back to Halifax alone, and become a
member of the family again.

The bemused lovers at last had to recognize that, for the
present at least, they had run out of options for continuing together. Lisa called her step-father back, told him she wanted
to return to live in Halifax and asked him to send her the
money for her air fare and a warm coat. The weather was
getting chilly, and Dennis had put all the rest of her clothes
into storage. (This was partly out of necessity; he had
recently taken in a lodger, David Sing-Woon Chan, who occupied the second bedroom in the apartment, and space was
limited.)

It can only be guessed whether there was as much relief
as sadness in Terry Turnbull's heart when he saw Lisa's plane
take off on her return to Halifax on October 4; his own statement conveys the impression that he did nothing to persuade
Lisa to stay with him. But she wrote him almost daily to say
how much she missed him—and also continued to keep in
touch with Dennis, asking him, among other things, to forward the parcel of clothing he had put in storage.

A few days later the tone of her letters changed. Dennis
should hold the parcel for the time being; the old family
quarrels had broken out again, and she could no longer
remain in Halifax. She was unhappy and confused, not knowing where to turn. She wrote to Terry in much the same vein.

On Tuesday, October 15, she was back at the Peterborough apartment, eleven days after leaving to start life

anew in Halifax. And two days later, on the Thursday, she was phoning Terry in the deepest distress. She found that she could no longer bear even to touch Dennis's hand, but Dennis was in such a wrought-up state she didn't like to think of what might happen if she were to leave him again, since he was once more talking of killing himself. (Quite possibly true, but speaking of the same period Dennis recalled that Lisa was also constantly distraught, running to hide every time the doorbell was rung. The lodger, David Sing-Woon Chan, who continued to be in residence, seems to have been unaware of any particular stress. But most of his evenings were spent taking dance lessons.)

One thing Lisa told Terry in that Thursday telephone call may have some possible significance. She said that if she could bring herself to stay with Dennis a little longer, "she would be able to make him see that she was not the person for him." Then, she declared, she would willingly make her life with Terry in Sudbury or anywhere else he wanted. Terry may have wondered whether his own wishes would actually have much influence on the course of events.

On the Saturday, October 19, the armed neutrality that the Goldings had established between themselves broke down. That evening, Dennis stormed in to their friends, the Evanses, in the next-door apartment to tell them that everything was finally over between Lisa and himself. Later that evening, he telephoned Terry in Sudbury to tell him to come down and take Lisa off his hands. For some reason, Terry hesitated before giving the least romantic of all excuses: he couldn't come right away because he simply didn't have the money to pay for the gas. He promised, however, to phone Dennis on Tuesday night to discuss arrangements. Lisa was at first furious that Dennis had called Terry, but the renewed tempest had an unexpected sequel to which Terry's stalling may have made a contribution—Lisa and Dennis found themselves discussing a reconciliation.

Sunday, October 20, was as sunny as their new mood, and the young couple spent the whole afternoon kayaking nearby at Eel Creek. They ate out, and on returning to the apartment, they did two things they had not done together for many months. They made love, and they conducted a civilized conversation.

Too much had happened for them to be able to live smoothly with each other immediately. Lisa needed, as she had needed in May, some space in which she could get her head together—but this time, without the distraction of any other man. Dennis, who had been doing so well in his new profession as a real estate salesman, must be able to concentrate on that for the time being, without having to worry about Lisa's welfare. With those sensible points agreed, they went to a loan company in Peterborough together on the Monday and arranged to borrow the $15,000 needed to finance their plans. Afterward they went to the movies and ate at a restaurant.

On Tuesday, Terry did not call as he had said he would. It was not until eleven o'clock on Wednesday evening that he phoned. It would be interesting to know what Terry would have had to say, but before he could say anything, Dennis told him gently that Lisa had decided there was no future in the kind of helter-skelter existence she had been leading with him that summer, and that she had realized that her feelings toward Terry "weren't that strong."

After a good deal of discussion, Lisa had finally decided she wanted to spend the winter somewhere down south, maybe Georgia. On Tuesday, Dennis had accordingly driven her down to the intersection of Highway 115 and Highway 401, and had last seen her on the ramp leading down to the westbound lanes of traffic on the 401, wearing her jeans and her backpack and expecting to hitch-hike all the way. She had said that she needed a little time to get her thoughts together, but he hoped that he would be able to join her later. Dennis added that it had been left that Lisa would call him in two or three weeks to let him know where she was.

That was October 23. Perhaps it was wounded pride (never since May had Terry been parted from her without re-

ceiving cards, letters or phone calls several times a week);
perhaps it was a somewhat guilty conscience that he had
stalled Dennis's plea to take Lisa away at once, and had
failed to keep his promise to phone on the Tuesday; perhaps
it was something in Dennis's story of Lisa's departure that
made him uneasy; for whatever reason it was, Terry felt im-
pelled to call Dennis again when only ten days had passed.
Dennis said he was glad Terry had called; he had heard from
Lisa four days ago. She was looking around for a place where
they could live, and was feeling fine.

Terry apparently said all the conventional things about
being happy if this meant Lisa and Dennis were going to be
able to make a go of things, and about Lisa's happiness being
his only concern, but added that he really would like to hear
from Lisa. Sure thing, said Dennis; he would ask Lisa to call
Terry the next time she phoned him. But that mightn't be for
another two or three weeks. Terry's phone call to Dennis was
on November 2, a Saturday.

Terry brooded over the weekend about what Dennis had
told him, and came to think it hadn't really answered any of
the doubts and uncertainties he had felt when he phoned
Dennis. So during the next week he telephoned Lisa's friend
in Ajax, told her of his concerns and begged her to concoct a
reason for asking Dennis herself where Lisa could be reached.
The friend did so, but before she could speak, Dennis had
demanded whether Terry had put her up to calling him. She
boldly lied, saying she simply wanted to answer a card Lisa
had sent her in October from Halifax. Then Dennis told her
Lisa was moving around too much to have a mailing address,
but she was definitely in Georgia, looking for a place where
he could move to after settling up his affairs in Peterborough.

Terry and the friend compared notes after this and
agreed the story sounded unlikely for a number of reasons,
the chief of which was the improbability of Dennis's so lightly
renouncing his thriving real estate career and its promising
future. In consequence, Terry phoned Lisa's mother in Halifax on Saturday, November 9. That lady was also equally

puzzled not to have heard from Lisa since her return from Halifax, particularly since Lisa's half-brother had been very ill when she left.

That same night, Lisa's step-father, who had been out hunting when Terry's call had come through but had been given all the details by his wife, called Terry back. In what sounds to have been a rather strained exchange, this gentleman made it icily clear to Terry that while he was glad Terry had brought the facts to his notice, he was not going to investigate them for Terry's sake—he frankly did not care if he never saw him again, and hoped Lisa would not either—but that he would do so out of his own very great concern for Lisa. Terry now wasn't to be shaken off so easily. "Regardless," he said stoutly, "even if Dennis and Lisa do get back together, I won't be satisfied until I hear it from Lisa."

As his first move on Sunday, Lisa's step-father went round to the police station in Halifax and confided the whole story to them, and a Halifax police officer was in his house, listening on an extension, when he telephoned Dennis to demand precise knowledge of Lisa's whereabouts. This time, Dennis's story was different. The truth was, he admitted, that he had no idea where Lisa was. He hadn't seen her from the moment he had left her on the ramp to Highway 401 nineteen days ago. She had walked right out of his life. He hadn't wanted her friends to know, but her parents had a right to the truth. He was worried sick about it.

When the call was finished, Lisa's step-father and the police officer exchanged looks. It would not be out of character for Lisa to have walked out on her husband; it would, however, be totally out of character for her to remain out of contact with her mother, her two brothers and her step-father all that time. She would have sent them some word of assurance.

As a sequel to that conversation, another police officer visited Lisa's step-father on Monday afternoon; Dennis had reported Lisa as a missing person to the Peterborough detachment of the Ontario Provincial Police just after noon. Ap-

parently regretting the stiff attitude he had taken in speaking
to Terry two days earlier, the step-father phoned him that
evening to report developments, which encouraged Terry into
coming down to Peterborough on Tuesday, November 12, to
make a long statement to the police and offer them any help
he could give them in solving Lisa's disappearance.

But also on Tuesday, Dennis was undergoing a searching
questioning in his apartment by Provincial Constable James
of the Peterborough detachment. It lasted a considerable
time. The next day, Dennis's step-father, at whose real estate
company he was employed, reported to the police that Dennis
had not turned up for work, and his telephone remained
unanswered. The apartment was empty; now both husband
and wife were missing.

In Dennis's case, not for long. On the following Saturday,
his local doctor reported that he had had a call from St. Vincent Hospital in Toledo, Ohio, to tell him that his patient was
receiving treatment for attempted suicide. He had been found
in rooms he had rented, unconscious from an overdose of barbiturates, with the room slowly filling with gas.

For what the reader chooses to make of it, the quantity
of barbiturates did not constitute a fatal dose (though not all
of us have exact knowledge of how many pills would be le-
thal), and the rescue was made by the landlord who was
bringing him furniture that he had promised to provide that
morning (though his arrival might well have been delayed).
The Toledo police were at once told of the circumstances,
and a police guard was set on Dennis in the hospital.

Meanwhile the Peterborough OPP had called in the assistance of the Criminal Investigation Branch of the Special
Services Division in Toronto. One of the first things that Constable James from Peterborough and Detective Inspector Bill
Perrin did on arrival in Toledo on the Sunday afternoon was
to make a detailed examination of Dennis's car. And on opening the trunk, they immediately saw, uncannily precise on the
flooring, the lipsticked imprint of a round, slightly opened,
mouth.

Not, as it proved, that much independent evidence of a crime would be necessary. Dennis, lonely and sounding tensed beyond control, had been talking half the night before with the friendly, worldly patrolman sent to guard him. At first it had purported to be the story of a friend, then Dennis would continue it as a first-person narrative, suddenly catch himself, and continue the narrative for the next few minutes as something that had happened to his unfortunate friend. In brief, it was the story of a man whose romance with a lovely girl had soured; he had spent thousands of dollars buying her every gift she had asked for; she had told him she loved another man, and in anger he had strangled her. He had buried her body where nobody would find it—but tantalizingly Dennis sometimes said it had been thrown into Lake Ontario, sometimes buried in distant farmland, and once, in a memory of his navy days, he said that "she had taken a 'deep six'"—and then added mysteriously that now his friend had to get rid of the automobile.

Having signed the necessary waiver of extradition, Dennis was brought back to Peterborough. That was November 19. He was now attempting to deny that the "friend" he had been talking about in Toledo was himself, and offered no guidance on where Lisa's body would be found. Indications that they had picked up from his various remarks led the police to suppose her grave would be found either on one of the farm properties he had sold in the area or on his stepfather's cottage on Chandos Lake, but even the use of dogteams failed to provide any sign of recent digging.

One week after his return, however, Dennis changed his mind after consultation with his legal advisers. Together with a statement, he provided a map showing the precise location. With its help, the body was found, as they had thought it might be, on the grounds of the cottage at Chandos Lake. But it had been buried about four feet deep in sandy soil, packed down completely level, and covered with leaves. After a five-week burial, Lisa still remained a macabre elegance.

In his statement, Dennis filled in the gaps in the pre-

viously known story from the time he and Lisa had eaten out
on the night of Monday, October 21. As it will be remembered, earlier that day they had taken out a $15,000 loan and
gone to the movies together. Lisa's plans for the immediate
future were to take a job and live in Ottawa, and over dinner,
Dennis had pointed out the advantage of living on a bus
route. This was not Lisa's picture at all; she had proposed the
purchase of a small, perhaps secondhand, car.

The discussion became more bitter later in the evening
when Lisa learned that Dennis only proposed that she should
be given $500 of the loan to get started; the remainder was to
be used as down-payment on a house in Peterborough.
They continued arguing after they were in bed. In a fury,
Lisa suddenly grabbed his shoulders, he said, and began
taunting him. He thought he was so smart; he had no idea
how much fun it had been making a fool of him. Making
flowers with Terry, she said (this, apparently was the Golding
term for the sex act), had always been much better than it
had ever been with him. And doing it with Terry had been a
real kick when Dennis had been so sure there was no hanky-
panky business between them.

She had always liked making a fool of him, because he
thought he was so smart. He might as well know now that
she'd been making a fool of him since back in Halifax, whenever he was at sea. When Dennis had screamed at her to stop,
she asked him if he had really thought she had enjoyed having sex with him the night before. She had loathed it, but she
had done it for one purpose. Now she was no longer tied to
the rotten deal Dennis had made her sign for the separation
deed. Now she was really going to take him.

That was when Dennis strangled her. There must have
been a struggle. There was blood on the floor, and either then
or later Dennis's thumb was fractured, but he recalled none
of it. He remembered only feeling frozen, with his hands
around Lisa's throat, for perhaps twenty minutes.

Afterwards, he had pulled her brown cord pants up over
her nightdress, put her suede boots on her bare feet, dressed

himself and then gone out of the door with her body in his arms. The serene lodger, David Sing-Woon Chan, slept undisturbed through all of this in the next room. The next scene is another nightmare. Dennis had to carry his burden down six flights of stairs, through the apartment building doorway and across a hundred yards to the underground parking garage. Dennis remembered falling downstairs twice, each time letting the body drop.

At last he had it in his automobile, but realized he did not know where he could take it. He drove around for three or four hours before deciding to bury her at the cottage on Chandos Lake. The ground was easy to dig, and he buried her deep in the ground. Clambering out of her grave, after arranging her neatly, he stumbled again and fell forward across Lisa's breast. When asked why he had chosen Chandos Lake for her resting place, he said with great simplicity that it was because it was so quiet and peaceful that he had thought she would like it. He loved her, he said, and always would.

Those who heard him could believe it; the tolerance he showed Lisa all through that summer, the many times he came to her assistance when she was only nominally his wife and the evidence that exists of his pleadings for her to return to him leave small room for doubt. There is, accordingly, a great temptation to end the account at that point, except that it would be a little bit too fanciful and not quite the whole truth.

When in Toledo, Dennis boasted freely to his police guards of the several conquests he himself had made. He might, of course, have been lying. But it is a matter of record, as well as a fascinating glimpse into the way human nature responds, that only hours after burying Lisa's body, Dennis was phoning a local girl of his acquaintance for a date that evening, and proposed at dinner that they should go steady now that his wife had left him. And that until he took flight she had been visiting his apartment constantly. That is how sad, lonely, frightened people really act.

Dennis Golding, sent to the Ontario Psychiatric Hospital at Kingston for psychiatric evaluation and found fit to stand trial, appeared before County Judge H. Deyman on a charge of murder on January 28, 1975. On the Crown's consent to accept a plea of guilty to the lesser charge of manslaughter, he was remanded for sentence until February 17. On that date he was sentenced to ten years, the first part of the sentence to be served at the Penetanguishene Hospital for the Criminally Insane where he was to remain until he had received sufficient treatment to allow him to serve the remainder of the sentence at Kingston Penetentiary. An appeal of this sentence was dismissed by the Ontario Court of Appeal on July 7, 1975.

There is just one footnote to add to the Golding story. When Inspector Bill Perrin opened the parcel of Lisa's clothing that had been put in storage in Peterborough, he found on top a printed receipt form completed in Dennis Golding's neat handwriting. It had been taken from the receipt book he used as a real estate salesman. It reads:

RECEIVED FROM: Mrs. Lisa Golding

Shit and abuse and very seldom a little love.

SIGNED: Dennis Golding

It could be Lisa's epitaph.

Curiouser and Curiouser!

"Curiouser and curiouser!" cried Alice.

Alice in Wonderland, *Lewis Carroll*

When the Second World War began, Arthur Williams had been a fifteen-year-old English schoolboy. Before it was over, he had become an experienced infantryman and a trained paratrooper. Clever with his hands, and with an active, versatile mind, he felt no urge to settle into any humdrum civilian job in a country where regulations, controls and rationing made civilian life almost as restrictive as it had been in wartime. So in 1947, at the age of twenty-three, he emigrated to Canada in search of freedom and opportunity.

He was short (five foot six), sinewy and lean, and ready to turn his hand to anything that presented itself. At the start, he went to Alberta where he seems to have had relatives, and for a while was vending ice cream for an Edmonton dairy. A succession of other jobs followed to keep him moving around, since he was too independent-minded to seek any steady employment.

In Wolf Creek, he met a Canadian girl, Margaret Mac-Donald, from Edson, Alberta, a couple of years older than himself. They were married in Edmonton. It may be guessed that the general feeling was that they matched each other remarkably well; they were both unconventional, offbeat characters, quite homely in appearance, with unusual hobbies and interests. She was a curio collector. He was a flying enthusiast and skyjumper. An enthusiasm they shared was for archery, at which they were both skilled; it may, in fact, have been this interest that drew them together. They remained childless.

Just how it was possible for this couple to have a fair amount of capital available a dozen years later is not known. A reasonable guess might involve an inheritance. In any case, in 1960 the Williamses moved further west to British Columbia—almost as far west as it was possible to get—since they purchased a five-acre property outside Ladysmith on Vancouver Island, about forty miles across the Georgia Strait from the city of Vancouver on the mainland. A two-family dwelling stood on the land; Arthur and Margaret took over one section, and found tenants for the other.

Their property investment left enough of their capital to launch another of their dreams: a bow-and-arrow factory. This was to grow from a mom-and-pop cottage industry located in their half of the duplex. Their hopes can be imagined. As a once fashionable sport, archery has been regaining popularity in recent years. Bow-and-arrow hunting has also become a recognized limited-harvest method of game management in many American and Canadian jurisdictions. With their own firsthand knowledge of an archer's needs, with their considerable manual dexterity and with practically non-existent overheads, they could expect to make not only the best bows and arrows in North America, but the cheapest.

All of which might well be true, but it would not have met with the success it deserved without an equally efficient way of reaching the public. Whether the Williamses were let down by their chosen distributors, or whether they had also expected the public to beat a metaphorical track to their door by means of mail order, is immaterial. Wherever the fault lay, the business never grew and drowned in a sea of debt in 1968.

With never enough orders coming in over those intervening years to keep Williams busy, he had been occupying
himself building a log-cabin-style house behind the duplex.
Its construction was completed in the year the business failed,
and he and his wife moved in to leave their half of the duplex
free for further tenants. He was a resourceful man. The rental
income was supplemented by odd jobs he undertook in the
neighborhood. Plainly, he was an energetic worker who
would seldom encounter difficulty in finding casual work. But
his mind remained set on higher objectives, and in 1970, he
embarked on a remarkable new project.

Singlehandedly, he began constructing on another part of
his property a three-story factory, looking vaguely like a traditional Swiss chalet. When it was completed, a sign proclaimed that it was the headquarters of the impressively titled
B. C. Institute of Mycology. He then announced his intention
of "developing a mushroom that could be grown on an automatic conveyor belt, and would contain no mercury."

A natural, in every sense of the word, for health food enthusiasts, who must certainly outnumber archery buffs. But
mushrooms can also provide more than a delicious accompa-
niment to a meal or a side salad. It is impossible to know
whether this thought was in Williams's mind when his
thoughts first turned to founding his B. C. Institute of Mycology. It is a fact, however, that in 1974 he was arrested and
convicted on a charge of making and trafficking in a prohibited substance, the mushroom-based hallucinogen methylene-
dioxy-amphetamine (MDA), popularly known on the streets
at that time as "the love drug." That conviction was overturned on appeal, but three years later he was charged with a
similar offense after a raid by the Vancouver drug squad.

On November 30, 1977, on the eve of his appearance in
court to answer this charge, he visited his lawyer, Sydney
Simons, in Vancouver to discuss his defense. The weather was
not favorable: nevertheless, Williams flew the comparatively
short hop to the mainland in the Cessna 172 of which he had
become a part-owner. (The other and probably larger part

belonged to the Inkster Aircraft Corporation.) By the time his consultation was concluded, the weather had worsened, but Williams was firm in his intention to fly back and arranged for flares to be lighted on the runway of Cassidy airport on the island.

Vancouver airport's Richmond Tower was monitoring his flight by radio and radar, and at nine-thirty that evening picked up his call stating that his automatic direction finder was not functioning. The tower at once offered him compass directions to allow his return to Vancouver airport, but Williams then said that he had just sighted the beacon and would not need help. A few minutes later, the light plane vanished from the radar screen, and the tower did not get a reply to their repeated calls. Arthur Williams had become a missing person. The following day, the log book, a life preserver and the seat from a light plane were found on the shoreline, and more wreckage was discovered later in December some distance away.

There cannot have been much question about the log book, but it appears that while nobody could say for sure that the other remnants were never a part of Williams's Cessna 172, nobody could confidently assert that they had been. Moreover, there were some who said they distinctly remembered Arthur Williams boasting that he knew how he could fake his own death if he wished. News of the disappearance was circulated, of course, but the only developments were the discovery of the additional debris.

If Arthur Williams had not had pressing reasons for a voluntary disappearance at that time, of course, the likeliest explanation was that his body and the remains of the Cessna were entombed in the silt somewhere near the mouth of the Fraser River. As things were, it was necessary to remember that he had had the training and the nerve to fly the plane low enough to escape radar beams and either jettison it far away, or across the few miles to the U.S. border. Neither course would be easy—but Williams was known to be a resourceful man.

Nevertheless, the law makes the presumption of innocence in the absence of sufficient contrary evidence, so when Margaret Williams petitioned the Attorney General of British Columbia four months later to call a coroner's inquest to allow her to settle the estate, the petition was granted. And after only formal evidence was given, on March 8, 1978, the jury declared her husband legally dead. He had not carried life insurance, but the Inkster Aircraft Corporation received, as well they might, payment on the policy covering the plane.

Margaret Williams had not shared in her husband's mushroom experiments. Since 1975, she had been operating a business of her own from a one-room log cabin on their property, trading in antiques, particularly glassware, rare old bottles and coins. Most of her sales were to summer visitors, and in other seasons she was sometimes gone for a day or so on the lookout for items to add to her collection. Usually she took her car and made her intention known to Arthur's sister, Ruth Dashwood, who had come to live nearby.

The two had met on Thursday, March 1, 1979, and according to Ruth Dashwood, Margaret Williams had said nothing about going on any foray and seemed her usual cheerful self. So when on the following Tuesday, March 6—almost exactly a year to the day from the date when Arthur Williams had been declared legally dead—Ruth Dashwood heard that her sister-in-law's car still stood outside her house, but that the house had been unlit and presumably empty overnight, she was sufficiently concerned to try to discover Margaret Williams's whereabouts. There was no sign anywhere; nobody had seen her since the previous day. At that point, Ruth wisely informed the local police.

At first the coincidence must have seemed too fanciful to try to make any connection between the two disappearances. Much more likely that Margaret Williams had simply taken it into her head to go foraging for merchandise. Investigations gave no indication that it was a planned departure for any length of time; only her cape and purse were missing, and the refrigerator contained spoilable food. Nevertheless, the

woman's disappearance had to be taken seriously in case she
had met with an accident or other misfortune. Her description was circulated across Canada and the United States, and
intensive searches were continued locally over an increasingly
wide area.

All to no avail. Weeks, then months, went by while the
usual sequence was followed; probable, possible, and then
not impossible locations were tackled, and still no sign or
clues. In August, when five months had failed to offer any indication of Margaret Williams's whereabouts, a news story
containing the essence of all this information went out from
the Canadian Press news agency to the media across Canada.
It supplied no conclusions, of course, and indeed added to the
mystery by revealing that a police search of the log cabin in
June had turned up a cache of $57,000.

Readers were naturally free to make of the story whatever they chose, but most probably agreed with the views of
Arthur Williams's nephew, an Edmonton golf pro, who said
he had never accepted the verdict declaring his uncle's death,
and openly wondered "if Arthur faked his death and later
came back to collect his wife, and if the two now are living
somewhere in seclusion."

Two weeks after the CP news story appeared, however, a
more detailed account of the perplexing mystery appeared in
the September 15, 1979 issue of *Alberta Report* from which,
by courtesy of its editor, much of this account has been
drawn. Far from explaining the two disappearances, it revealed that the state of affairs existing on the Williams's estate
at the time of Arthur's disappearance was even more puzzling
than supposed.

Although Arthur Williams had moved into the log cabin
house with Margaret in 1968, it had not been for long. In
1970, just about the time that the B. C. Institute had been established, he moved out. The Williamses had split up. All the
property was signed over to become Margaret's sole property.

Their emotional separation from each other at this point
may or may not have been vast; obviously, there are two

theories. Certainly, the actual physical separation of this
strange couple was, although significant, surprisingly small.
Arthur took up co-habitation with another woman in one section of the duplex building just in front of the log cabin, of
which Margaret now became the sole resident. Arthur presumably became her tenant.

This arrangement continued from 1970 until the time of
Arthur's disappearance in 1977. The other woman, however,
remained a fixture in the duplex. She did not move away until
a month after the disappearance of Margaret Williams in
1979.

A piquant detail. The police search of the log cabin in
June 1979 had been as a consequence of an anonymous tip-
off, and the considerable amount of currency found—the
exact amount was $57,300—had been neatly wrapped and
placed inside a yellow plastic pail. A further revelation. A
careful examination of the three-story factory led to the discovery of a tunnel running underground about a hundred
feet, emerging at a point out of the line of vision from the
factory. Its sole purpose could have been for drainage. But it
did not escape the observation of the policemen that it was
wide enough to accommodate the girth of an agile and wiry
five-foot-six entrepreneur seeking a discreet method of entry
and departure.

Selecting the items that best suited them out of this un-
matched variety of facts, it is likely that ten different fiction
writers could come up with ten plausible explanations. An ingenious long-term double vanishing act, as the nephew
suggested? Perhaps. But why leave so much money behind?
Two separately planned disappearances with no intention of
reunion? Perhaps. But again, there's that money. One death,
accidental or planned, and one disappearance, also planned or
involuntary? Rather too coincidental for easy credibility.

Two other factors should be borne in mind, although to
some extent one cancels the other. Although the Crown may
have had a stronger case against Williams in 1977 than the
one they lost on appeal in 1974, a man facing the same charge

in 1977 received a sentence of only three years and would probably serve considerably less. Presumably Arthur Williams's solicitor would have been able to forecast a likely maximum sentence of this magnitude. To most people, the risk of such a fate might not appear so onerous as to justify such an elaborate, costly and dangerous hoax.

On the other hand, there are those boasts Williams made about being able to fake his death. He sounds the kind of man who would relish the chance of having a justification for making good his boast. Is a man who stakes everything on starting a bow-and-arrow factory on an offshore island in the Pacific Ocean a man likely to weigh the consequences of his actions with careful deliberation?

Asked if he had any personal theories on the mystery, Sergeant Robert Udahl of the RCMP in Ladysmith smiles. "Plenty," he says. Adding, "But I don't think that at this point any of them would hold up." That, of course, is the fascination of this case. Evidence is available to throw doubt on every speculation.

Yesterday's Headlines...

Girls of sixteen or even nineteen in the 1940s and 1950s may have been less sophisticated than the average fourteen-year-old today. Nevertheless, it is doubtful that the demure, domesticated, church-going creatures described in reported disappearances of those days were really as unworldly as contemporary news editors presumably imagined their readers wanted to believe.

For all the stiff official jargon old police reports and statements contain, the young women who take shape out of those dusty files are somehow more vibrant and believable. After spending an hour or so staring into a hooded microfilm reader, spinning through the magically recreated pages of old newspapers, it is easy to imagine the sound of their giggling behind one's shoulder, sharing the amusement of seeing how the progress of some of those stories were handled by the press.

During months when other exciting news was scarce, a young girl's unexplained disappearance could be made more than a nine-day wonder. The longer the disappearance lasted, moreover, the more sentimental became the image presented of the missing girl, and the more sensationally imaginative the treatment of the story. The two that follow are representative of several more.

The Crumbacks lived in the west part of Toronto with their three children, Mabel, Bruce and Gary. In 1950 Mabel was nineteen, Bruce thirteen and Gary eight. On the last weekend of May, Mr. and Mrs. Crumback drove to Detroit to attend a wedding. Bruce was away. Because her little brother had to be looked after, Mabel's activities were restricted, so she invited a boyfriend, Jim Bryan, to call round on Saturday evening.

After Gary was in bed, Mabel started flirting with Jim. She was a small girl with black wavy hair; lively and animated, she had the glow of youth. She was two years older than Jim Bryan, and appears to have amused herself by teasing his inexperience.

On Sunday morning, her eight-year-old brother woke late, and finding the house empty, concluded Mabel had gone out for a walk. After a few hours, he grew hungry and raided the refrigerator, although he knew Mabel was to have given him a midday meal.

He became increasingly worried as the afternoon and evening went by and the house remained empty. His parents did not return until half an hour before midnight, and Gary was still up. On learning that he had not seen his sister since the previous evening, they called the police immediately. All of Mabel's day clothes at first seemed to be still in her room; the only garment apparently missing was her pajama top; the pants were found neatly folded under the pillow. Later, an aunt recalled a skirt Mabel had sometimes worn; that, too, proved to be missing although nobody knew whether it had been there on Saturday.

Questioned, Jim Bryan said that he had left the Crumback house half an hour after midnight of the Saturday, and evidence apparently supported this. A neighbor reported seeing the side door ajar, and lights on in the kitchen and in Mabel's room at about two o'clock, and Gary thought he remembered being awakened at some such time during the night by one or more male voices. He was also sure that when he had gone downstairs on Sunday morning he had found the kitchen door open, although it was normally kept shut at night to confine the cat. Mr. Crumback added, rather surprisingly, that his daughter had no housekey and, although it was presumably the day after payday at her office, he was able to state she had no money.

In the following week, the disappearance of Mabel Crumback was front page news across the province. The original $300 reward was increased to $1,000 in the next week, and the following Saturday's papers were enlivened with the news of a reported sighting. An automobile containing "several people" had stopped outside a tourist camp in Ancaster, about forty miles away, and someone was certain of seeing Mabel Crumback "lolling in the back seat"; her black hair had been dyed blond, the witness said, and she "appeared to be drugged."

Two days later, another witness was sure he had seen Mabel outside Brantford, this time "lying on top of a haystack" some hundred yards away. Search parties were organized, and a hundred soldiers took part in them. In one way or another, the Crumback disappearance stayed on the front page for two weeks, when it was pushed further inside newspapers by the appearance of a "killer-bandit" in Langton. A few days later, Harry Truman ordered U.S. planes and warships to go to the aid of South Korean forces, sweeping both Mabel and the killer-bandit out of the news altogether.

Nothing has been heard of Mabel Crumback since. Today, over thirty years later, it would be pointless to do more than remark that it would require a wholly incredible scenario to provide an explanation taking account of all the evidence provided in the Crumback case; some of it was certainly false or undependable. Which parts those are remain a matter of speculation.

The last male known to have seen a missing girl inevitably becomes an early target for suspicion. The Crumback disappearance had a close parallel in this way three and a half years later, also in Toronto.

In contrast with her shy and retiring only brother, Marion McDowell was the tomboy of the family, boisterous and outgoing. They lived with their parents in the east end of the city where she had opportunities to indulge her love for tennis, swimming, roller-skating, loud music, pinball alleys and, particularly, the company of boys. She had started earning her living when she was fifteen and, after holding jobs for a short time in a department store and a bank, became an invoice typist a year later for a big downtown printing firm.

She had been dating from her schooldays, and had had one affair more serious than the others when she was fifteen. From her diary, it was later found to have lasted nearly seven weeks, but although she had special favorites since then, she always kept as many options open as possible. She was something of a headhunter; by the time she turned seventeen in November 1953, she had painted in red nail varnish on a white enameled chair in her room the first names of some twenty boys she had dated.

A few weeks after her birthday she ran across a nineteen-year-old youth, Jimmy Wilson, a scaffolding rigger, she had met on a couple of occasions during that summer, and they went for a drive that evening in his 1942 five-passenger Plymouth coupe. Apparently they enjoyed each other's company enough to go out together the following day, a Saturday, and then made a similar date for the following evening, Sunday, December 6.

Wilson called for Marion at seven that evening, and they drove further east. Marion had at first suggested driving some twenty-five miles to Oshawa, but they settled for a quiet road only a few miles into Scarborough. They probably both knew the location since the other cars parked off the roadway all held other similar-minded couples. According to Jimmy Wilson, he parked at about seven-forty, switched off the engine, turned on the radio and gave Marion a cigarette. They both lit up, and after a little conversation, started necking.

He hotly insisted that he had not even attempted to have intercourse because he was "sure Marion was not that kind of girl," but whatever degree of intimacy had been reached was interrupted about two hours later he said, when the passenger-side door was flung open, and he found a flashlight shining in his eyes. Then a voice barked, "This is a stickup!"

This, he related, was not such an alarming experience as it might sound since it followed a style of humor popular with youths of the neighborhood; possibly he and Marion had been victims before. Nevertheless, when he saw a gun pointed at him, he obeyed the next instruction to get out of the car.

He could only see what the watery new moon revealed, but the bandit appeared to be about five foot eight, with a balaclava mask pulled over a sharp, narrow face. There was nothing distinctive about his voice, but the handgun, from Wilson's description, could have been a Walther .38 or a Luger. The bandit told him to hand over his wallet, and he obeyed. It contained a ten-dollar bill. The bandit then told him to turn around, and knocked him out with two fast blows to the back of his head which later required seventeen stitches to close.

He recalled brief moments of consciousness when he was in the back seat of his own car with the girl's body sprawled across him; the car was in motion with the bandit at the wheel, then blackness returned. His next recollection was of finding himself alone in the car, now parked three lengths behind another in a yard he did not recognize. He saw someone—presumably the bandit, but he never turned—close the trunk of the second car, enter the driver's seat and drive off. Clambering back into the front of his own vehicle, he had to decide whether to give chase or make his escape. Unarmed and still unsteady, he put the car into reverse and drove around until he could find his way home along a road that he recognized.

After hearing his story, his father took him immediately

to the Scarborough police station to repeat it. Before ten-thirty that evening the search for Marion McDowell had been started. Still bleeding, Wilson was able to direct the police to the yard where the second car had been; it proved to be part of an unoccupied private property quite near the point where he had been assaulted. Later investigations showed that to gain access the bandit had broken locks and cut through a chain put in place only hours earlier.

Wilson's wallet was found discarded near the spot where the assault had taken place. Midway between where the two cars had stood in the yard, the police found a bar of old-fashioned laundry soap, wrapped in its outer packaging but with its inner wrap removed. It seemed to have had brief use; the lettering embossed on the soap was still clearly legible.

The interior of Wilson's car, particularly the back seat, was drenched with blood. Some of it was his own A-type, but most was O-type, and presumably Mabel's. (One of her parents had O-type, the other A; hers might have been either.) The head scarf she had been wearing was still in the car with cuts indicating that if she had been wearing it folded as Wilson had described, she had sustained a heavy head blow. The amount of O-type blood found in the car raised the strong possibility that she was already dead before her body was taken from the back seat.

Reports of the disappearance drew 2,000 volunteer searchers; airplanes and two helicopters joined in. A scuba diver went down a well, and fingerprint experts dusted Wilson's car. Thanks to the white enameled chair and its nail-varnished trophy list, all of Marion's previous dates were traced and questioned at length. All without result.

Simply as the last person known to have seen the girl, Jimmy Wilson could not avoid being the subject of popular suspicion. But street talk went further. What had he and Marion, who had not seen each other for the past few months, found to talk about at such length in those two days before her disappearance? What was the explanation of that bar of Sunlight soap, recognized standby of the back-street abortionist? To many, the theory of a botched abortion made more sense than the mysterious-hooded bandit. Although these theories were not published, the same possibility had occurred to the investigators. The only direct evidence that Marion McDowell was not pregnant (from a female relative who recalled the girl's mention of painful menstrual cramps in the previous month) was anecdotal and unverifiable.

On the other hand, none of Marion's group of friends had any evidence to the contrary. Moreover, Jimmy Wilson did not prove to be a particularly intelligent or quick-witted youth. He held adamantly and with apparent sincerity to the same facts he had given within hours of the girl's disappearance in repeated interrogations by different trained investigators.

If any other person known to Wilson had played a part in the disappearance, some indication of it could be expected to have emerged, but Wilson showed no sign of discomfiture at any time during his questioning. Taking account of the fact that his head wound, which had required seventeen stitches, could not possibly have been self-inflicted, they finally concluded that he had told them the exact truth. In the hope of silencing the persistent rumors, Wilson was taken to Buffalo for a lie-detector test, and the press announced that his truthfulness had been scientifically established.

Perhaps the way in which disturbing disappearances are handled by the media provide sociologists with as much of a sidelight on the times in which they occur than do the actual disappearances. The Marion McDowell case remains one of the most remarkable. The following August, more than eight months after her disappearance, the Toronto *Telegram* (now deceased) decided to stimulate its summer circulation by sponsoring a visit from the celebrated Superintendent Robert Fabian of Scotland Yard to find the vital clues the local police had missed. Fabian, just retired after an indisputably distinguished career, was then engaging on a North American tour to promote his recently published memoirs.

Whether he expected to have any success, working on a

cold trail without his usual trained team to assist him, or
whether he simply felt the accompanying publicity would be
helpful in selling his book, it is hard to say, but he accepted.
The police—since January of that year, coordination of the investigation had been undertaken by the Ontario Provincial
Police—treated the famous visitor with respectful but cautious courtesy, fully aware that the *Telegram* was determined
to wring a front-page story a day out of Fabian's comments,
theories and possible discoveries, even if it entailed retreading
old ground once again.

Fabian did nothing to add to his lustre. It is said that at
the end of his career he no longer possessed all the concen-
tration and drive he had demonstrated in the past. Perhaps it
is only legend that at one conference he seriously inquired
what the autopsy had revealed about the contents of the missing girl's stomach. His unproductive stay lasted into September when he renewed his publicity campaign for his book in
the United States.

Disappearances generate a hysteria of their own. In the
weeks after Marion McDowell vanished, local youths drove
their jalopies around the streets at night with girl friends pre-
tending to yell in terror for help. The McDowell family telephone rang constantly with calls from people claiming to be
the abductor. The Toronto *Star*, consulted by police in
confidence to arrange publication of a coded personal message to contact an alleged kidnapper with a ransom demand,
did so, and—it would be nice to think, as a result of an edito-
rial misunderstanding—made that fact public on its front
page. Nobody, of course, showed up to collect; since there
was no further attempt, it can be assumed to have been a
hoax. An elderly lady reported seeing the missing girl, her
face contorted with terror, being driven at great speed
through a back street in an automobile with a strange creature more animal than human at the wheel.

One more footnote is appropriate.

Considerable derision was extended—reportedly, by Superintendent Fabian, among others—toward Jimmy Wilson's

account of the so-called bandit's behavior; what kind of robber, it was asked in effect, takes the money and, although fully disguised, throws it away and proceeds with an apparently senseless killing?

The answer, of course, is a kind for which robbery is not the important motive. In this case, possibly just an effective way to get the youth to step out of the automobile. Five years earlier, a repeated offender known as the Red Light Bandit gained notoriety in California from his use of a flashing red roof-light on his car to frighten the male from a parked car before knocking him out, and compelling the girl to engage in oral sex in his own car. (By a technicality of Californian law, the forcible removal of the girl from the first car constituted kidnapping, punishable by death. It may be recalled that Caryl Chessman was convicted as the Red Light Bandit, and after a bizarre delay of twelve years, was executed in 1960, although he had taken no life.)

Perhaps more comparable were the killings accredited to an unknown individual who came to be known as the Moonlight Murderer in Texarkana, Texas. There, in February 1946, a young couple were listening to their car radio late one night of a full moon, when the car door was swung open and the youth was struck on the head. The girl was knocked unconscious as she tried to escape, and was raped.

A month later, a young salesman and his girl, parked only a mile from the same spot, suffered even more tragically. He was shot through the head at point-blank range; she was shot twice and mutilated before being raped. At the next full moon, a seventeen-year-old youth was found shot and killed, a mile from the car in which he and his fifteen-year-old girl friend had been necking; her body was found near the car, shot, mutilated and raped. The following month another moonlight murder was committed, but only the man was killed. His wife escaped to call for help. The Moonlight Murderer is believed to have been a never-identified man who jumped under a train on the tracks outside Texarkana a few days after this last killing. (A description of the case is con-

tained in *The Encyclopedia of Murder* by Colin Wilson and
Pat Pitman, published in England in 1961 by Arthur Barker
Ltd.)

In the Marion McDowell case, then, the sequence of
events described by Jimmy Wilson—behavior almost certain
to be outside the comprehension of a not overbright nineteen-
year-old rigger—conforms quite closely to a recognizable pattern. There were only two differences. First, the assailant
probably struck the girl with considerably greater force than
he intended, and the youth with less. And second, he presumably succeeded in disposing of her body. Which, as many
chapters in this book make apparent, does not present much
difficulty in Canada, even for a novice.

...Today's Back Pages

Times change. In the early post-war years, there was a euphoric feeling that a better, safer world of tranquil harmony had been created, now that peace had been restored. The sudden disappearance of a young girl from a respectable middle-class home was an affront to the senses, an occasion for hysteria. One revolutionary generation later, little of that feeling endures in the public mind. A disappearance may sometimes make front-page news the following day, but in the absence of significant later developments, it is not the kind of story a modern news editor is tempted to keep alive with artificial respiration.

Yet the two stories that follow are as typical of the times in which they occurred as are those of Mabel Crumback and Marion McDowell in the previous chapter.

The first concerns four people of much the same age. Susan was nineteen and a half, but Bob had turned twenty that week. Debby and Steve had both celebrated their twenty-first birthdays that summer: Debby only seventeen days earlier, in fact. Although they all worked for the same automobile agency in Toronto's Islington district, they had not dated before that Friday, August 11, 1978.

At lunch everyone agreed it would be a good night to go dancing. As Susan, Bob and Steve all lived in Mississauga, they would start from there. They would use Debby's car because she would be driving home to Willowdale when the party ended. Susan and Bob finished work before the other two, so Steve and Debby would pick them up at their homes about eight. They all liked Susan's idea of going to the Ports of Call, and Steve suggested they could finish the evening with a drink at his home, since his parents were away on vacation. Everything seemed set for a lively summer evening.

According to plan, Debby drove Steve home to Mississauga at seven o'clock in her 1976 Cordoba, very sleek with its maroon body and white vinyl top, and spent a few minutes freshening up while he changed out of the suit he wore for business. Debby had no need to change. The black halter top with the white-and-yellow skirt she had worn to work was equally suitable for dancing. She was, as always, ornamental: the halter top provided a background for her two slim necklaces. When she danced, people would notice her gold wristband and the two gold rings, one set with an opal, the other with a small diamond.

They reached Bob's house around eight after making a detour to pick up a bottle of whisky at the liquor store on Applewood Plaza. Bob invited them in, and since Susan was not expecting them until a little later, Steve, Debby and Bob chatted for some fifteen minutes while sharing a joint. Not an orgy; just the ritual with which tens of thousands of young Canadians would probably be celebrating the start of that weekend. It is notable, incidentally, that these three made no attempt to persuade Susan from her somewhat staider ways during the evening.

Having time to spare, they drove to a service station to fill the Cordoba's gas tank on their way to Susan's home where they chatted for a few minutes with her parents, and left about nine. By the time they reached the Ports of Call on Yonge Street, and parked, the place was already crowded, so they returned to the car and drove to Friday's Tavern on Eglinton Avenue East and parked again. Luck was still against them. After standing in a line that never moved in the five or ten minutes they waited, Debby suggested they should leave her car where they had parked it and walk the fairly short distance to the Camelot Tavern just on the corner on Mount Pleasant Road.

It was busy, as all such spots are on a Friday night, but they found a table reasonably close to the floor where the next three hours could be spent dancing. A little drinking, too, of course, impossible now to know exactly how much, but Steve estimated it later as perhaps three to five apiece. If so, a probably imprudent but not astonishing amount of alcohol over a three-hour stretch. As a guess, Susan and Bob were probably the most moderate. Whether or not this was true, after they returned to Debby's car, it was Bob who took the wheel for the drive to Mississauga.

Debby sat beside Bob in the front, with Steve and Susan behind. Steve invited the others to come back to his home to continue the party, but at this point Susan declined because, she told them, her parents had imposed a curfew. They drove her home first, and she went inside after they all sat for a while in the car in the driveway saying their good-nights.

Bob then drove Steve and Debby back to Steve's home. It was a little after two. Inside, Steve opened the bottle of whisky purchased earlier, and he and Bob had a drink together while Debby made herself a cup of black coffee. They sat chatting awhile, and Steve played some records on the stereo. About three, Steve, the good host, left Bob and Debby to themselves and went downstairs to amuse himself practicing pool shots until four o'clock, when he heard them moving around, apparently preparing for departure.

Bob did not have far to walk home, but in view of the hour, Steve told Debby she was welcome to stay in the spare room until morning if she wished. She declined with thanks, explaining she had to get home, bathe, dress and pack in readiness for a weekend visit with friends who had a cottage up north. The night had become chilly, however, and she wanted to drive home with all the windows open to stay alert. She would accept the loan of a wrap.

VICTIM

Eleanor Joan GOLDING

Top side: Lisa Golding ("A Summer Affair") Courtesy of the Ontario Provincial Police

Middle: Dennis Golding. The story of a man whose romance with a lovely girl had soured. Courtesy of the Ontario Provincial Police.

Bottom: Exhumation of Lisa Golding's body from her sandy lakeside grave. ("A Summer Affair") Courtesy of the Ontario Provincial Police

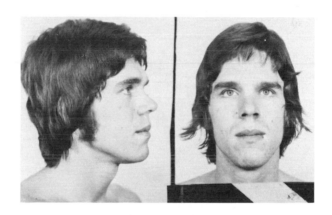

-REWARD-

GIRL MISSING

MARION JOAN MACDOWELL

Believed Kidnapped from this Municipality Sunday December 6th 1953
by an armed man.

DESCRIPTION

Age 17 years: 5'3": 130 lbs: Blond Hair: Blue Eyes: Round Face:
Good Teeth: Wearing white blouse, with black or blue trim; Black
Wool pleated skirt: Black Ballerina shoes: Silver chain bracelet,
with heart on right wrist, and a ring on left hand initialed "MM"

I am authorized by the Board of Police Commissioners, to offer a
reward of $1000.00 for information leading to the arrest, and
conviction of the person, or persons responsible for the disappearance of the above mentioned person.

Should there be more than one claimant for the above mentioned
reward, which expires at Midnight February 28th 1954, they will be
apportioned as the Board of Police Commissioners deems just.

Kindly have all possible enquiries made in your District, and
forward any information to this Department, COLLECT.

Telephone PLymouth 5-1121 and AMhurst 1-2570

Township of Scarborough
Police Department
2001 Eglinton Avenue East,   W.G. McLellan,
Postal Station "H"   Chief Constable.
Toronto 13, Ontario

*Reproduction of the original reward poster issued following the disap-
pearance of Marion McDowell. ("Yesterday's Headlines") Copyright, reproduced by kind permission of the* The Globe and Mail, *Toronto*

Top: Deborah Silverman
("...Today's Back Pages")
Copyright, Canapress Photo
Side: Sharon Drover ("...To-
day's Back Pages")

Top side: Grace Todd. She frequently swore that one day she would really leave the man....("Continental SuperFreeze Model 507") Courtesy of the Toronto Metro Police

Bottom left: David Todd ("Continental SuperFreeze Model 507") Courtesy of the Toronto Metro Police

Bottom right: Detective Sergeant John Leybourne inspecting Continental SuperFreeze Model 507. ("Continental SuperFreeze Model 507") Courtesy of Sergeant E. Pollock

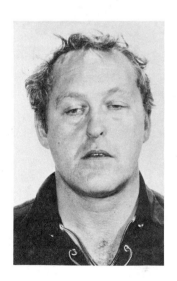

Steve had just the thing, a heavy blue-and-white-check sports shirt. She admired it, adjusted it loosely around her neck, checked her purse for her keys and, by the time they had told each other again what a great night it had turned out to be and wished each other a good weekend, it was four-thirty. She had not had a drink since leaving the Camelot Tavern more than three hours ago, and to Steve and Bob, watching her drive off smoothly, she seemed in good shape.

Neither imagined he would never see Deborah Silverman again.

She made the journey safely. There is ample evidence of that. Her car was neatly angle-parked in its regular space in the northwest corner of the parking lot behind the apartment building on Bathurst Street where she and her mother lived. Evidence, too, that she must have walked the thirty or forty steps it would have taken her to reach the rear door on the north side of the building, which provided the closest access from the parking lot.

The door was always kept locked but could be opened by any of the tenants with their front-door keys and, by way of a long, narrow corridor, led directly to the foyer and elevators. The passage was twenty-six feet long but only two feet wide, making it difficult for two people to pass. It can be imagined as an eerie, empty space, especially before sunrise at a little after five o'clock in the morning. Unfortunately for Debby Silverman, it was not as empty as usual at the moment she entered that Saturday morning.

An hour later at six-fifteen one of the tenants, a man of twenty-nine who had to go to work early that Saturday, unknowingly came upon evidence that something peculiar might have been happening in that corridor. Intending to use the rear door to reach his automobile, he noticed two broken necklaces lying on the corridor floor about two feet inside the doorway, along with a purse. He picked them all up and returned, with curiosity and a little titillation, to his apartment to examine his find. The purse apparently contained nothing of value, to his admitted disappointment, only keys, miscellaneous accessories and its owner's name and address in the same building.

Deciding to keep the two necklaces to see if he could mend them, he returned only the purse to the corridor floor where he had found it. In doing so, he saw another object he had not previously noticed: a torn pair of panties. Modesty prompted him to stuff the panties into the purse and return upstairs to Debby's apartment and knock discreetly on the door. Receiving no answer, he left the purse on the doorstep and, now late for work, finally made his departure, no doubt meditatively.

The purse remained undisturbed outside the third-floor Silverman apartment until eight that morning when it was observed by the young son of another of the tenants. He rummaged through it with similar curiosity, but apparently left it as he had found it. Irrelevant evidence? Very probably. It seems most unlikely that Debby and her assailant were acquainted. The remote possibility exists that Debby's purse had once contained an indication of how somebody who knew her habits and might have been lying in wait. Whether that remote possibility can be dismissed depends on the shrewdness of the investigating officers in assessing the testimony of the two individuals known to have examined the purse and in satisfying themselves that the contents were not seen by other eyes. This purse incident—which a fiction writer could furnish with three or four believable explanations—is worth noting as representative of the amount of evidence that must be sifted over and over again to make certain that all possibilities have been explored.

The morning absence of an intelligent, socially active twenty-one-year-old daughter after a late-night party is nothing to occasion more than mild concern to a level-headed modern mother, certain that the telephone will soon ring to explain the circumstances. Probably several hours of frustrating attempts to reach Debby's friends on a Saturday morning went by before Mrs. Silverman realized that something was seriously amiss. It is unlikely that much time had elapsed after the discovery of the purse on the doorstep (might she have expected to find a ransom note inside?) and the parked car before Mrs. Silverman telephoned the police emergency number at two-thirty. Officers from the thirty-second division were around within minutes since the circumstances were unquestionably alarming.

A Saturday afternoon in high summer is a bad time to try to make inquiries because so many people will be away both from their homes and their usual places of employment. By nightfall, however, they had not only learned the strange history of the purse and secured the return of the two broken necklaces (one of which had already been repaired), they had also interviewed all the tenants who were not away for the weekend or on vacation, and found further broken strands of Debby's necklaces just outside the rear door in the car park. Beside them were two shirt buttons later positively identified as having come from the checked shirt Steve had lent her. Nearby was a Band-Aid, but there was no certain way of associating this with the missing girl or her assailant.

Her mother was, of course, able to identify the necklaces and provided a detailed description of the other jewellery and the clothes Debby had been wearing, down to the "off-white, high-heeled dress shoes with narrow strap, size 8 or 8½."

An intensive investigation was started. Steve, Bob and Susan (those are not their real names) were taken repeatedly over their evidence about how and when the party had been arranged and required to help in reconstructing every minute of its progress. All the tenants of the building were separately interviewed concerning their own activities of that Friday night and those of visitors they had received. Past and present members of the automobile agency staff as well as its management were questioned exhaustively. Various lines of inquiry suggested themselves; all seemed to lead to dead ends.

At five forty-four on the morning of Monday, August 21, nine days after the disappearance and at about the same time that the assault originally must have occurred, someone phoned police headquarters and delivered the abrupt message: "You're never going to see Debby Silverman again." Before the caller could even be asked to give a name, the line went dead but, like all messages received, the call had been taped.

The caller appeared to be an adult male with no perceptible accent, who either possessed, or had assumed, a pronounced stutter. There was no way to establish whether it was a sick-minded hoax, but all the investigating officers listened to the voice in case they encountered it again or could detect a similarity with that of anyone already interviewed. Another blank. On August 24, Toronto Metro Police issued notice of a $5,000 reward they had been authorized to pay for information leading to discovery of Debby Silverman's whereabouts. It was not claimed.

The full-scale investigation continued through the rest of summer and into the fall. Then, on a clear, fine Sunday, November 12, precisely three months after the disappearance, eighteen-year-old David Smith took a noontime stroll through a wood lot on his father's farm. It occupied the southwest sector formed by the intersection of Highway 7 with Durham Regional Road 13 in Brock Township, about forty miles east of North York. Young Smith paused to take a closer look at something odd but at first unidentifiable sticking out of the ground where animals had been digging. Getting closer, he had the stomach-turning experience of recognizing that it was part of a human foot.

He hurried home and told his brother. They decided to await their father's return from church, since he would be due in a few minutes. As soon as Smith heard of David's grim discovery, he telephoned the Ontario Provincial Police detachment at Beaverton. His call was received at one o'clock, and within thirty minutes the first two OPP officers, a corporal and a constable, were on the site. After their first report was received in Beaverton, further officers and the coroner were dispatched, and after the news had been relayed to Toronto, Detective-Inspector M. K. Macmaster of the Criminal Investigation Branch arrived to take charge at about quarter to seven.

Disinterment of the body had had to proceed with great care since it was in an advanced stage of decomposition. Digging consequently had to be conducted at some distance from where it was judged the rest of the body lay. Partially exposed, it was covered with a thin layer of the surrounding soil, and additional care was taken to preserve all the soil removed in large canvas sacks. By the time Detective-Inspector Macmaster had arrived, the sun had long set, and the work had been continued with the help of illumination supplied by a portable generator operated by volunteers from the Brock Fire Department. It must have been an eerie sight.

It was not before eight-ten in the evening that digging had been completed, photographs taken and exact measurements made. Then a body board was gently slid at a cautious distance below the corpse, and the whole makeshift catafalque enclosed in a standard police body bag for transportation to the pathologist in Toronto. Only a foot of soil had been covering the rest of the body when the discovery had been made.

Detective-Inspector Macmaster organized a painstaking search of the area surrounding the burial site the following day, but nothing indicating any possible connection with the crime was found. In Toronto, the Provincial Forensic Pathologist, Dr. J. Hillsdon Smith, was having what was in some ways an equally frustrating experience since the advanced stage of decomposition not only rendered visual identification impossible, but precluded any prospect of determining the cause of death.

There could be no doubt that the young female had been the victim of a criminal assault because her hands were found to be tied behind her back with the sleeves of a blue-and-white-check shirt. Her halter top was around her neck, but her brassiere was hooked and in place, and the white-and-yellow skirt was fully zipped. She was shoeless.

The likelihood that the body was that of Deborah Silverman had, of course, been recognized since its discovery had first been reported, and by now it was virtually a certainty. Verified identification came when the forensic dental specialist was able to confirm that an x-ray of the jaw showed a perfect match with the detailed charts provided by Deborah Silverman's own dentist.

In mystery fiction, discovery of the body in such dramatic circumstances would inevitably have provided a bizarre clue leading to the killer's arrest. Regrettably, things only rarely work that way in real life. In this case, although the disappearance had been reported early, although it had engaged the full-time attention of a crack team of investigators, and although the autopsy was conducted by one of the most knowledgeable pathologists in North America, it was not even possible to say for sure that she had died by violence. For all the autopsy revealed, her heart might have failed, she might have choked to death on her own vomit, or death, it might be suggested, could have resulted from a drug overdose.

The torn panties and the tied hands suggest a particularly nasty rape, and the disappearance of the gold bracelet and the two jewelled rings indicate a practiced thief. But whether it was a rape-murder or her death was unintended, or even whether it occurred in the building, remain unanswered questions.

The choice of the grave site does not necessarily argue in favor of the killer's having familiarity with Brock Township. Highway 7 East is only a few miles farther north up Bathurst Street, and the obvious choice for someone wanting to reach a secluded rural area as quickly as possible. The wooded area at the intersection of Highway 7 and Durham Regional Road 13 may simply have been the first suitable location encountered. Time, too, was probably getting short; it would soon be sunrise by summertime.

On the whole, it seems that the killer would be more likely to choose territory where he was not known by sight in order to avoid recognition on the road, or recognition of his automobile while he was engaged in burying Deborah Silverman's body. One point of interest in that connection, though,

is the implement he used to dig the ground. Had he found a
spade or a fork somewhere in the grounds of the apartment
building? Did he carry digging tools in his automobile in
summertime for any reason? Did he call somewhere on the
way where he could pick them up? The only alternative explanation, however unlikely, is that the act was premeditated.

In any such case, of course, her assailant would have
been guilty of criminal assault or worse, but there was nothing at all to provide the investigating team with a positive
clue. None of the hundreds of people they had already questioned in connection with the girl's disappearance had any direct link with Brock Township or any nearby part of the
Durham Regional Municipality. The investigation continued
on a major scale until the following spring, when many of the
officers concerned were switched to other assignments. The
case of Deborah Mildred Silverman remains open.

One month after the discovery of Debby Silverman's
body outside Toronto, another young girl vanished from the
streets of St. John's Newfoundland. Like Debby, Sharon
Drover was attractive and socially active; unlike Debby, she
was a high-school dropout, well known to the juvenile courts.
Because of Sharon's unsettled family life, her childhood and
short adolescence are matters of public record; on the other
hand, we can assume that Debby's was a normal, uneventful
development from youth to young adulthood against a well-
educated middle-class background. Conversely, Debby's disappearance received widespread publicity and became public
record almost immediately. Sharon had been gone for over a
month before anyone decided to determine whether she had
disappeared by choice.

She was one of the three children of a couple living on
Bell Island (population: 6,079) in Conception Bay on the At-
lantic side of Newfoundland. It was an unhappy home, and
when Sharon was seven or eight, she, her brother and her
sister were made wards of the court and placed in foster

homes. So many newspaper stories have appeared telling of
hapless children in similar circumstances who, apparently
through no fault of their own, have been transferred from one
set of foster parents to another that it is worth noting that
Sharon had the more fortunate experience of spending almost
all of the remaining years before she was seventeen in the
care of a motherly woman in St. John's who was fond of her.

But Sharon was not the woman's only charge. The foster
mother may not have been a strict disciplinarian, but it is far
from certain whether things would have turned out better for
Sharon if she had been, because Sharon responded badly to
discipline. Her foster mother seems, in fact, one of the only
two adults toward whom Sharon showed a liking; when she
had passed out of the foster mother's care, she kept in touch,
calling round at what had been her home for half her life for
a talk about old times and to give a guarded account of her
activities.

As a child, though, Sharon was a handful—at home, in
school and on the streets of St. John's. She was a bad student
and a frequent truant, she was wayward and she kept bad
company; it was her way, apparently, of impressing those of
her own age group and getting the attention of older girls and
youths. Predictably, playground drugs became part of the picture quite early, and another word soon being used about
Sharon was "promiscuous."

She grew to become a well-built girl of five foot five,
with blue eyes and long brown hair; not really beautiful, but
attractive enough to be a prize winner in a beauty contest in
her high school years when she was sixteen. Not the first
prize. The second or third, so far as people can remember.
But she dropped out of school in the ninth grade. She never
had any close friends.

She had been in and out of trouble with the youth authorities off and on frequently since she was fourteen because
of what are officially known as "behavioral problems"—
chiefly, it seems, connected with her ready sexual availability
—but she must have been treated with leniency. Everyone

agrees she was fundamentally a good-natured, rather immature young girl, simply wanting to be liked.

Eventually, however, after she had dropped out from
school, the time came when it was realized that something
would have to be done about Sharon; she would soon be seventeen, and in danger of acquiring a criminal record when
her behavior resulted in a charge brought against her as an
adult offender. In the summer of 1978, she was accordingly
ordered to undergo assessment and treatment in the psychiatric department of the Health Science Hospital in St. John's.

It was there that Rosemary Lahey, then a social worker
for the hospital, came to know her. Rosemary Lahey is a
friendly young woman of great composure and few illusions
about her clients. "There was nothing mean or vindictive
about Sharon," she says, "but she was in a rebellious mood
when she arrived. She insisted she needed nobody's help, she
could look after herself. It was kind of sad and ridiculous, because the more she demanded to be treated as a responsible
person, the more childish she became."

After a while, Sharon began opening up more to Rosemary Lahey, telling her she still often saw her brother and
sister, although they had all gone their separate ways. "Somehow she was sure they were all going to be reunited with
their parents one day in a kind of paradise regained. I don't
think it had any resemblance to what her early life had really
been like or what any of them were like today. In that way
she was almost frighteningly immature, but she was easy to
like."

Someone else who became friendly with Sharon that
summer was Stephen, a fellow patient in the hospital at the
time, just short of nineteen, and very much into rock and po-
etry. He too was touched by her vulnerability, but alarmed to
find that his casual friendliness was at once welcomed as a
sexual advance. Sharon, apparently, always came on strong,
"always wanting to be hugging and kissing, but I just never
saw her that way." One day she told him that as soon as she
left the hospital she was going to get married; "it was to this

guy she'd just met two days before who she'd met when he was visiting another patient." Some visitors smuggled in weed or pills; Sharon apparently was willing to try anything going.

The notion that friendship did not necessarily imply constant cuddling and more was probably unfamiliar to Sharon, but after a few days she accepted Stephen as her special friend, spending part of every day talking to him. Nothing deep; about music, about her early life, about school, about her prize in the beauty contest . . .

Stephen left hospital before Sharon did, but he had given her his home phone number, and for the first few weeks she called him frequently. When the time came a few weeks later for Sharon's discharge, it became Rosemary Lahey's responsibility to find her suitable living accommodation. "I wasn't too happy about the boardinghouse I had to put her in," she says now. "It was a clean, efficient place, but it was run by someone who was too much of a disciplinarian for Sharon at that stage. She'd had treatment, she was now seventeen, and I'd like to have seen her somewhere where she had the opportunity to show she had gained a little bit more self-control. But there's such a desperate shortage of suitable accommodation, it was the best I could find."

Rosemary Lahey continued seeing Sharon as frequently as her always heavy case-load allowed. She found time as well to call on Sharon's foster mother; both women were anxious for the girl to start her adult life in a more productive way. The next time she saw Sharon, there was evidence, either for good or bad, that she had determined to start living her own life. She had moved out from the boardinghouse where she had been placed, and moved into rooms—the first living accommodation she had ever found for herself—downtown, on Livingstone Street.

Next came the good news that she had found herself a job, working at McDonald's on Kenmount Road, in the western part of St. John's. It had been the first job interview in her life, and being accepted had given her a feeling of real accomplishment. This, says Rosemary Lahey, was the top point

in Sharon's life to date. It was part-time shift work and the
wage, of course, was low, but it was the first money she had
ever earned and a job she enjoyed. She was never late and
never missed a day. She also phoned Stephen to give him the
news early in November, and he says she had never sounded
happier.

Something she did not tell Rosemary Lahey or Stephen
at this time was that an eighteen-year-old youth was now living with her. This was someone she had met at a "halfway
house" or transition home where she had been visiting another acquaintance in temporary residence. Imprudent, perhaps, but Sharon always needed to feel wanted. And, so far as
is known, it worked well enough. She seemed generally cheerful at work and continued arriving in good time each day despite the long walk it entailed in the increasingly cold
weather. Inevitably, news of the resident boyfriend reached
Rosemary Lahey who felt uneasy at the thought that the arrangement might set back the progress Sharon had been making, but she recalls that the only advice she found she could
give was "Sharon, whatever you do, please take care of your-
self."

That was early in December, a busy month for a social
worker. Sharon had ceased to be on Rosemary Lahey's official
case list since her seventeenth birthday, so they did not meet
at any appointed times; Sharon, though, had got in the habit
of dropping in for a chat every few weeks, or if she did not,
Rosemary Lahey would make time for a call. She was far
from sure that Sharon was mature enough emotionally to assume responsibility for her own well-being without occasional
encouragement, and she had become interested in the girl.

Several times during the month she found herself thinking of Sharon, but was too busy with her official case-load to
do anything about it, and then had come Christmas and the
New Year. So it was some time in January before she was
able to act on her impulse. But she drew a blank, both at 9
Livingstone Street and at McDonald's. Sharon was no longer
living on Livingstone Street and had not turned up for work

at McDonald's since December 28. More surprising still, her last paycheck had never been collected.

At least, it had surprised Rosemary Lahey more than it had McDonald's; they had apparently resigned themselves long ago to the fact that those bright, cheerful teenagers who staffed their restaurants so efficiently when they were there could not always be depended upon to be there when they were needed. Unexplained and unannounced absences were too frequent to be a major concern, and weeks often went by before ex-employees picked up a waiting paycheck. Certainly Sharon had been a good timekeeper, but after all, she had only been there less than two months. And a lot of people went away over the New Year.

Rosemary Lahey realized that this indeed could be true; there could be half a dozen explanations with someone as impulsive and harebrained as Sharon was still capable of being. Nevertheless, the situation was so potentially disturbing that she knew she could never dismiss it as being one less problem to worry about. So she had to fit some part-time detective work into her schedule. Her first inquiry, to Sharon's one-time foster mother was not reassuring. Sharon's boyfriend had also been to see if she knew where he could find her; he had not seen her since Friday, December 29, when she had left Livingstone Street and set off for McDonald's.

None of the young people working at the restaurant knew where she might have gone; none of them had become a close friend in the two months that she had worked there. None of her old acquaintances had seen her, neither had her brother. Even this negative information had taken time to develop, and Rosemary Lahey realized there was none further to be spared. So on Tuesday, February 13, 1979, she finally took her worries to the police station, and the official investigation was started—forty-six days after Sharon Drover had last been seen. The trail, of course, was cold, although not much colder than it had been when Rosemary Lahey became aware of Sharon's disappearance.

The policing of Newfoundland is somewhat unusual. Be-

fore it joined Confederation in 1949, all of its island and
mainland territory was covered by the Royal Newfoundland
Constabulary. Today, as in all the other provinces except Quebec and Ontario, the Royal Canadian Mounted Police provides
urban and rural police services across the province—except,
in this case, in St. John's, the capital and by far the largest
city. Here, the Royal Newfoundland Constabulary still exists
under its original title and retains sole jurisdiction, proud of
its traditions.

One of these, as it happens, is a consistently good record
in the finding of missing persons, even higher than the high
national average. This probably owes something to the fact
that Newfoundlanders are friendly, sociable folk, observant
and interested in the activities of the people around them,
and to the other fact that the Avalon Peninsula, on which St.
John's is located and which is the home of about a third of
the province's total population, occupies less than a thirtieth
of the total land area of Newfoundland. In other words, less
room to get lost and more people to keep an eye on you.

"Usually, the only disappearances we don't clear up in a
matter of days at the outside are drownings, and that's usually in the wintertime when the tides are tricky," Detective
Inspector Stan Waterman says. "This is a busy ocean port,
and men do go overboard in accidents occasionally, and their
bodies may not be found until months later. But otherwise,
disappearances are rare. We hadn't had one like Sharon
Drover's for years, nor one like it since."

Cold as the trail might be, therefore, they were confident
that someone would remember seeing Sharon recently, or
would know something about her present whereabouts. Naturally, as usual, the boyfriend who had last seen her came
under close questioning, but even apart from having apparently nothing to gain and a good deal to lose by her absence, his innocence and genuine concern seems to have been
fully established.

The girl had left 9 Livingstone Street at about half past
three on December 29 of the previous year dressed for her

walk to McDonald's in blue jeans, knee-high black boots and a white T-shirt with "YMCA and YWCA" stenciling on the front; she was wearing a long beige coat. That much seemed to be certain, but it proved of no help. The youth said she had seemed quite cheerful when she left, and she had spoken to him of no worries on her mind. But he knew she could be impulsive, and could behave erratically; he had really only begun to be concerned when he had heard nothing from her after some days, and the rest of her clothes remained in the closet.

Detectives from the Royal Newfoundland Constabulary went over the same ground that Rosemary Lahey had covered, but more thoroughly than she had been able to do, and extended their inquiries further, but with no greater success. As soon as it had seemed there was no simple explanation for Sharon's disappearance, photographs and the scant information available were given to the RCMP Divisional Headquarters in St. John's and also to local newspapers and broadcasters. In due course, details were entered on the computerized Canadian Police Information service (CPIC), so as to be available to police forces across the country as well as the United States. But for all the response any of this brought, Sharon Drover might have opened the front door of 9 Livingstone Street that cold December day and walked straight into the fourth dimension.

Spring came, and slowly the snow disappeared. The weather improved and suddenly, as always, it was summer again and the temperature steadily rose. Children could run and play happily in spots that only weeks earlier would have been bleak and inhospitable. On the second Sunday of June, two twelve-year-olds from the Pleasantville area were exploring on top of Cuckhold's Head on Signal Hill, just outside of St. John's. A breeze was blowing off the sea, hundreds of feet below, and as they approached the cliff, they became aware of an unpleasant, heavy odor.

Curious, they ventured cautiously forward, and looking over the cliff's edge, saw what at first looked like a heap of outer clothing on a ledge about one third of the way down. It was, of course, a body although no limbs were visible.

It was then seven-thirty in the evening, and by the time news of their possible discovery reached the Royal Newfoundland Constabulary, it was getting dark. Lieutenant Miller was on the scene fast to verify their story, the truth of which was all too evident, and realized that recovery of the body would present some problems and would have to be undertaken in daylight.

A recovery crew drawn from the Constabulary and the St. John's Fire Department was organized that evening and went into action early on Monday morning, June 11. It was not a pleasant task nor one that could be done quickly; it involved the lowering of four men by ropes over the sheer edge of the precipice, and the men had to be equipped with gas masks and shovels. The body was arranged as gently and carefully as possible in a body bag which was then drawn up by ropes. At noon, an RCMP helicopter took the remains directly to the Pathology Department of St. John's General Hospital.

Lieutenant Miller, who had been part of the recovery crew, says, "All we could see was that it was the body of a girl, but we all assumed it would turn out to be Sharon Drover, because she was the only local girl to be missing for so long. It looked as if she had died of exposure. She'd pulled the collar of her coat up over her head, and drawn up her knees, to get all the cover she could. Made me think of a robin in a snowstorm."

Exposure it probably was, although the pathologist's report, issued the same day, properly refrained from conjecture. It stated only that "cause of death [was] not demonstrated in markedly decomposed body of young, adult, white female . . . No evidence of foul play demonstrated."

But the surprise was that it did not appear that this could be the body of Sharon Drover. Whoever she was, she had not dressed in the clothes Sharon was described as having been wearing when she was last seen; a ring on the finger of one hand was of greater value than anything Sharon had owned; two photographs in the coat pocket had backgrounds that did not seem to have been supplied by anywhere in Newfoundland. The photographs, in fact, appeared to have been taken more than three thousand miles away, in Calgary, Alberta, where Sharon knew nobody and had never been.

Moreover, the bone and body structure of the corpse on the ledge were those of a fully grown woman, probably in her twenties, rather than of a girl of seventeen.

Sharon Drover, in short, was still missing, and the Royal Newfoundland Constabulary had on its hands the body of an unidentified woman.

Despite the photographs, it might have taken a considerable time less than twenty years ago to identify the body, but thanks to the computerized CPIC system mentioned earlier, in this age it is possible to narrow the possibilities rapidly by consulting the data on the physical characteristics of all missing persons of the same sex, within the apparent age group, and of the approximate height as that of an unidentified body. (Always provided, of course, that the individual's disappearance has been reported and that an accurate description has been obtained. Two cases defying the system are described in the chapter "Remains in Doubt.")

In this instance, since the condition of the body made it certain that death must have occurred at the very least some months earlier, and the photographs indicated the possibility that the young woman came from Alberta, the search could be even further narrowed. Dental records soon provided verification that the body was that of a young woman of twenty-four whose disappearance had been reported by her father in Calgary in February—by a blind coincidence, almost on the precise day that Rosemary Lahey had reported Sharon Drover's disappearance in St. John's.

What had happened to the young westerner could never be established as a certainty. So far as could be discovered, she knew nobody in St. John's, nor had visited the city before. Later it was learned that she had visited a small Catholic church near Signal Hill the day after she had last been seen in Calgary, and that after spending some time in meditation and or prayer, she had departed quietly, without exchanging any conversation with the caretaker. She had left behind some personal possessions, which the caretaker had been looking after, expecting her return.

Her purpose in going to the cliffs overlooking Cuckhold Cove has to remain uncertain. It may be relevant, though, that her father reported that rock climbing was one of her favorite sports, and that she was an experienced winter climber. Had she incapacitated herself in an accidental fall? Possibly, but the autopsy report mentions no broken bones.

Or had she intended to take her life? Possibly again, but as Lieutenant Miller asks, "If that's what she was after, why would she have stayed on that ledge to die of exposure, when she could have ended it so much faster by jumping the rest of the way? It seems likelier to me that she slipped climbing down to the ledge because it was icy and hurt herself too badly to climb back to the top. Perhaps she was just resting till she felt good enough to try, and the cold made her lose consciousness. But we'll never know."

But what of Sharon Drover? Nothing has come to light to explain her disappearance. If she was the victim of an unknown killer who hid her body, not only has it never been found, but no similar crime has been discovered. If she acted on a sudden impulse and ran away—to start a new life, to escape her boyfriend or escape the consequences of something she had done—Rosemary Lahey, who probably understood her better than anybody, declares that the only certainty she has is that Sharon could not be alone; she simply did not have the resources to operate independently in an environment she was not familiar with.

"She would have been calling her foster mother or me within the first few days," she says. "But I'd be quite prepared to hear she met some guy who stopped to give her a ride that day, and talked her into going with him to Toronto or Montreal or Vancouver, and said he'd give her money for new clothes. If after that, he ditched her, we would have heard from her soon enough, of course, wherever she was, but what I could believe is that she fell in with a pimp who set her to work on the streets. As a matter of fact, with new clothes and more money than she could make at McDonald's, and somebody to run her life for her, she might not be unhappy at all. In a way, I'd prefer that to be the answer than any other realistic alternative."

Stephen, on the other hand, takes a more romantic view of her disappearance. In the winter following, he composed the words and music for a piece he called "A Song for Sharon," which went:

> Every time I close my eyes
> I wonder where you are;
> I wonder just how you are
> Because you're my star.

Refrain:
> Did you mean to run away?
> Do you think you're gonna stay?
> Will you make it back some day?
> 'cause your life shouldn't be this way.

> Ever since you were a child
> You were never loved;
> No one seemed to care for you,
> They just pushed and shoved.

> I hope I see you again sometime,
> In this life or the next;
> I know you're no longer here,
> But I hope for the best.

(Refrain)

Continental SuperFreeze
Model 507

The notion that young Grace Todd might not in all circumstances be perfectly well able to look after herself does not appear to have occurred to anyone but her office friends. As a rather odd result, her complete disappearance in 1971 failed to become a matter of public record until some four months after they had tried to raise an alarm.

Grace Todd had started with the North American Life and Casualty Company in Hamilton when she was seventeen-year-old Grace Filman. She was always trim and alert, and she proved to be bright and reliable; an office treasure able to be trusted with responsibility as she became more adult. In the next few years, in fact, perhaps her only seriously questionable action was to marry David Todd, then twenty-five, on August 17, 1959, thirteen days after her twentieth birthday.

Without knowing what the two people concerned are hoping to find or trying to escape, the reasons for many marriages are often mystifying. This was certainly one. With a formal education that ended at the sixth grade, and with no particular manual skills or mental agility, the bridegroom's prospects were unpromising. They had notably worsened when he received a suspended sentence for theft when he was twenty, and a sentence of six months definite and three months indefinite on another charge of theft when he was twenty-three.

Somewhat short and already a little overweight, he was not impressive physically. His features were saved from the commonplace only by being slightly lopsided, his voice was weak, and he was not an entertaining conversationalist. He was, however, totally, irrevocably and jealously in love with Grace Filman. Perhaps that was enough for her at twenty. Interestingly, though, active sex does not appear to have played any important part in their marriage; even as a lover, David Todd was unremarkable.

Whether or not it was what she had unconsciously sought, it cannot have taken the young wife long to know she would have to be the head of the family. Her position in the insurance company continued to improve, and when she learned its quarters were going to be transferred to a newly constructed office tower in a densely populated residential-commercial sector of Toronto's Don Mills suburb in 1965, she did not hesitate. She and David would move to allow her to stay with the company. The Todds accordingly moved into a one-bedroom eighth-floor dwelling on a back street of high-rise apartment buildings off the Don Mills Road within minutes' walk of the new offices. (Their apartment was at 1 Deauville Lane; adjoining streets have names like Grenoble Drive, Dufresne Court and Vendome Place. The names suggest a richer and more glamorous ambience than the reality provides.) Grace by then was nearly twenty-six, David thirty-one.

Six years later, Grace had become supervisor of the mailing and filing sections. David was unemployed. He had not found work until a year after their move, and after the Dunlop tire factory in Toronto closed in 1970, he had made little effort to find steady employment. In May 1971, Grace Todd took a one-week's leave to treat him and herself to a trip to Jamaica for his thirty-seventh birthday, but by then the strain of their peculiar partnership was showing.

If Grace now acted as more of a mother than a wife to

David, her role was by no means that of a patient, loving parent. David, indeed, must have been exasperating. Beer drinking and idleness had increased his weight to two hundred pounds, and his manner had become a compound of subservience and jealousy. Irrationally convinced that Grace spent time with a lover when she was supposed to be at her desk, he telephoned her several times a day to check on her. His calls, and Grace's barbed replies, were something of an uneasy joke she shared with her office friends. She frequently swore that one day she would really leave the man . . .

Most of his day was spent idling. His hobby, significantly, was weaponry, so some time was occupied cleaning and fondling an astonishing collection that included two double-barrel shotguns, an antique flintlock, a couple of nineteenth-century European army rifles, a .22 Cooey single shot rifle, a .32 caliber revolver, a .22 caliber revolver, two pellet pistols and a crossbow. In the season, he occasionally went hunting with Patrick Todd, one of his brothers. In the summer, he spent hours hanging around the swimming pool at the rear of their apartment building.

Surprisingly, this habit resulted in his obtaining an odd job of sorts. Walter Drakeford, a contractor with a number of different interests which included operating that and another swimming pool on St. Dennis Drive nearby, was plagued by vandals who entered the pool areas after dark. He decided it would be worth hiring someone as night-watchman; Todd, who seemed to spend so much of his time there anyway, was an obvious prospect. It was the kind of job Todd could handle, not much work and very little traveling. He said he would "help Walter out," and started work about the middle of June.

He now rose later. Most afternoons, he drifted up to the Mississippi Belle where Grace could be expected to join him after she had left her office.

The Mississippi Belle stood almost next door on the Don Mills Road to the tower in which the insurance company had its office; its bar represented the evening watering hole for

many of the workers and residents in that crowded little
world, and its regulars formed another group familiar with
the Grace and David relationship. Several of them came to
know the couple quite well in the casual way that bar ac-
quaintanceships become established, but none of them felt
greatly concerned when the pair ceased coming, although one
of the regulars did later have an amusing bit of gossip to tell
the others. But bar acquaintances do not assume responsibility for each other's movements or behavior; etiquette
requires the reverse. To them, Grace was simply the bright
chick (brighter still with her recently blonded hair and her
deep suntan after her Jamaica vacation), with the lively line
of chatter and wisecracks, and David was the paunchy husband who never took much part in the conversations.

"Did he just sit there, disapprovingly?"

"It was more that he didn't seem to know much about
any of the things or the people we were talking about. And
when the conversation got away from him altogether, he
would probably get up and wander about the room, or go and
get himself another drink."

"Would you say you all drank a fair amount?"

"Well, we were all there for an hour or two most evenings, so I guess you could say we did. Only beer, though, for
most of us. That's all Grace and David drank, anyway. But
since he was usually there before the rest of us, and often
went off to order another glass for himself, I'd say he was
generally drinking three to her one."

"Did they quarrel?"

"He didn't, although he was sometimes in a bad mood if
he suspected her of anything. Told me one day she'd brought
some flowers home he thought she'd had from a boyfriend,
and he'd thrown them away. Another time, he said that if she
ever really tried to leave him, he'd shoot her. But he was
crazy about her."

"How about Grace?"

"Well, she kidded him a lot about not having a real job,
and often asked him how long he thought she was going to go

on keeping him. Same way she needled him about putting on weight. Used to call him Hippo or Pearshape sometimes. But he'd just sort of grin, like it was a family joke."

At the end of July, Grace was entitled to two more weeks of vacation. As she had told her office, she and David proposed to go camping. To allow for the August holiday, she left the office on the evening of Thursday, July 29, telling them to expect her back on the morning of Monday, August 16. But she failed to return.

It was quite unlike her to be absent without explanation, and the first thought they had was she and David might have met with an accident on their return journey. One of Grace's friends, Florence Millar, who was also a section supervisor, phoned her home number. The call was answered by David Todd, who gave her the surprising news that Grace had "left him for an older man," and that he had no idea of her whereabouts or future plans.

This naturally astonished Florence Millar. It was not that she believed her friend's marriage was running smoothly; everybody knew of Grace's impatience with David; her frequent threats to walk out on him may have sounded to be half-joking, but they had been made. On the other hand, Florence had never heard of any middle-aged or other boyfriends being seriously involved with Grace. More to the point, she could not imagine Grace deserting her job, or leaving her old friends in the lurch, without a word of advance warning. Troubled, she reported the circumstances to Ralph Pettyjohn, one of the company's vice-presidents.

Pettyjohn was equally perplexed, though unsure what they should do about it. Perhaps they would be hearing from Grace Todd shortly; if not, perhaps they could talk to a member of her own family. But succeeding days brought no news from or about the missing employee, and nobody knew the names or addresses of any of her relations. So some days later, the vice-president consulted the police about reporting Grace Todd as a missing person.

This proved to be a more ticklish question than it might

seem. As it was explained to him, when married people suddenly vanish, they probably have reasons that are not police business. In this case, the woman had apparently spoken of leaving her husband, and since it sounded as if the husband would be the loser if she was his meal-ticket, there seemed no reason he would want to get rid of her. People had a right to complain if the police start prying into their personal lives without good reason at the request of outside parties. Her family would almost certainly know if Grace Todd had really disappeared. That was why, when the person concerned was a responsible adult with family members nearby, the police felt that disappearances were best reported by a close relative.

In fact, in cases such as this, the police officer has to exercise his discretion because circumstances can be so varied. Nothing that Ralph Pettyjohn was told was incorrect, but the trouble was that even though Grace Todd did have a mother living in Burlington, and a married sister living in London, Ontario, they were not an especially closely knit family.

Grace's mother had received a call from her daughter in July to let her know she and David were going camping for the first two weeks in August, but although Grace had added that she would be getting in touch with her again before the end of that month, her mother was not worried when this vague promise was not kept. Grace's sister in London rang the Don Mills number once for a chat but, receiving no answer, simply decided to call again another day. There was nothing of importance to discuss.

So it appears the first person outside Grace's office circle to be aware of any changes in the Todd household was one of the regulars at the Mississippi Belle who saw David Todd come into the bar one afternoon with a girl who was a stranger. Todd and the girl passed by him without a word of greeting to take seats in another part of the room. Thinking that David should be away with Grace, he was curious enough to move over to their table in a few minutes on the pretext of giving a friendly greeting. David mumbled an in-

troduction—which went unremembered—and confided that
he was "out for this girl's mother."

Since the regular was now quite intrigued by the mystery
and knew where the Todds lived, he called round a few days
later and knocked on the door. Todd opened it only wide
enough to identify his caller. Seeing who it was, he whis-
pered, "Look, you'll have to go away. I've got a naked girl in
here." His visitor left. It was a great story to tell the others,
but clearly nothing that needed to be reported to the authorities.

Whether Todd did in fact have a female visitor is not
known. But a married lady who lived with her husband on
another floor of the same building later reported the heavily
flirtatious attention Todd had been attempting to pay to her
and other women at the swimming pool in August. She and
her husband had known both the Todds, and for some reason
the couples had ceased to see each other since the previous
February; she had accordingly been astonished when the first
thing Todd said to her was that he had good news: Grace had
gone to live with her parents in the States. For one thing, she
knew no reason why Todd would think she would welcome
the news; for another, it was incomprehensible, since Grace
had previously told her that her father was dead, and that her
mother lived in Burlington, Ontario.

But other changes in Todd's behavior were no less remarkable. Previously his attitude to the teenagers in and
around the pool had been decidedly hostile; he had yelled
down from his balcony when their noise had interfered with
his morning sleep. Now he not only cultivated their friendship
but seemed to be trying to copy their ways of dressing and
talking. Before long, the two pool lifeguards had moved in to
share his apartment, and shortly after that, the apartment became an open house for a small horde of other teenagers. He
offered himself as their friendly counsellor, confessor and all-
round pal. In return, they refrained from prying into his own
private life; it was clear enough he had a secret grief, but he
had given so many different explanations of his wife's ab-

sence, nobody was sure what the truth was. To some he said she was living with her parents, to others that her employers had sent her on a training course to the States and to others he had confided that she had left him for another man.

To one of the older youths, nineteen-year-old John Moore, who lived in one of the townhouses across the way in Vendome Place, he elaborated on this. Although his wife had left him, he said, they were still very much in love; actually, the night before, his Grace had come in quietly through the door and kissed him gently and silently before departing again. Later, John Moore remained convinced David Todd was somehow sure this had actually happened to him, and that it was a treasured recollection.

His youthful visitors were invited to drop in at any hour, examine his firearm collection and help themselves to anything they fancied in the refrigerator. Only one item was out of bounds, the Todd freezer. This was a fairly compact appliance, white enameled, some fifty inches wide, thirty-three inches high, and twenty-eight inches deep: the Continental SuperFreeze Model 507.

Plugged in but untouched, its lid was held down with adhesive tape. Inside, Todd explained, was a testing device to check the appliance for leakage. It was faulty, he said, but the guarantee would be void if anyone tampered with it. But no serviceman ever seemed to come to check the readings.

Summer ended. The swimming pools were closed, and the contractor who had employed Todd as night-watchman now paid him to deliver auto parts and haul garbage. The money was more than handy; although the lifeguards had returned to school, other local teenagers continued to be his guests, and for the first time in twelve years Todd was now having to fend for himself. Even with these earnings, the rent went unpaid. But as Grace had written a check for the August rent in advance, and the Todds had been steady tenants for a long time, the management showed forbearance for a while; the lease on Apartment 807 had until the end of November to run.

As winter approached, Todd's loneliness and need for acceptance apparently became greater. Out on his deliveries, he sometimes picked up teenage girls in the street, told them wild stories, and made what seem to have been ineffective and half-hearted attempts at sexual intimacy. For a short while, a girl with a considerable record of drug usage and juvenile delinquency slept in the apartment; her stay coincided with a confused report to the police station of the theft of most of his gun collection (but not the .22 Cooey rifle), and later of his automobile (which later appeared either to have been returned or not to have been stolen at all). It is not impossible to believe her statement that during her stay, she and Todd slept separately.

From time to time, Mrs. Filman remembered she had heard nothing from her daughter Grace since the end of July. She phoned once or twice unsuccessfully. She wrote, and her letter was unanswered. When she wrote again, her letter was returned, marked "Not known." None too pleased, Mrs. Filman concluded that the Todds had moved without bothering to let her know, and she conveyed this to her other daughter Eva in London.

Eva was puzzled; Grace had always been independent, but although she also had phoned Grace unsuccessfully a few times, the number had at least seemed to be in service. She accordingly kept calling until her brother-in-law finally answered one day. This was on Saturday, November 27. David expressed mild surprise that she had not heard from her sister; Grace had left him, he said, on her birthday, August 4. She had bought a lot of new luggage, and had been picked up by a man he did not know, and they had driven off in a green car. Before she had left him, she had told him that she would be getting in touch with her mother and her sister when she had settled.

Eva called her mother at once to relay this astonishing news, but the same evening Mrs. Filman also had a call from David himself, who said he would be visiting her the next day. He duly arrived, expressed his great regret at Grace's lack of consideration in not keeping her promise to keep her own family informed and confessed that Grace's departure had actually put him in an awkward situation. She had ordered all these new clothes and luggage before she left, but had left it to him to pay the bills . . . He would certainly take responsibility for them, and he expected that Grace would be getting in touch with all of them soon and would be able to pay him the cost, but the store was pressing him for full payment. Was there a chance Mrs. Filman could lend him the money? He drove back from Burlington with Mrs. Filman's check for $420, leaving behind his promise that he would repay the loan at a rate of $50 every month from January.

Desperation had prompted the act. His lease would expire in two days' time, and it had not only been made clear that this would not be renewed, but that until the arrears had been made, his possessions could not be removed. Mrs. Filman's check would solve that problem, but he also had to find somewhere else to live. Further ahead, there would doubtless be other difficulties: repayment of the debt to his mother-in-law, answers to her inevitable questions about Grace, payment of rent to his next landlords, what he should do with the freezer . . . But Todd knew little was gained by crossing bridges before coming to them. Time always provided answers, sooner or later.

One possibility occurred to him, in fact, just by looking out of his apartment window. There, less than a hundred and fifty yards away were the townhouses on Vendome Place, where young John Moore lived. Through John, he had become friendly with Cathy and Charles Cassidy and Layne Jackson, Charles's girl friend, as well as with their good-natured and easygoing mother, Elise Cassidy. John was often over to Townhouse 11 at 4 Vendome Place where they lived, and they seemed able and willing to accommodate visitors at short notice. Not the long term solution, perhaps. But a temporary answer, anyway.

It worked. True enough, he had to tell Mrs. Cassidy that the arrangement would be only until the end of the year, and that he would be getting rid of most of the contents of his present apartment. When the time came, in fact, most of the articles he decided not to take were shared between John Moore and the others helping with the removal, so they found their way to Vendome Place anyway. But nobody wanted the clothes he said Grace had left behind after buying herself a new wardrobe, so all her personal possessions were bundled into plastic bags for the garbage.

Even so, clearing out the apartment took longer than they had reckoned; the move was spread over three nights. Cleaning out a desk drawer, they came across American Express checks issued to Grace Todd for a total of a hundred and sixty dollars in U.S. funds, apparently left over from their trip to Jamaica in the previous May. They already carried her specimen signature, of course, but David Todd pocketed them; providence was already at work unexpectedly providing answers.

Finally the job was finished. Much to Mrs. Cassidy's dismay, since her space was strictly limited, the final load included the Continental SuperFreeze, which Todd had insisted must be handled with special care. With resignation, Mrs. Cassidy indicated where it might be placed in her living room. As soon as it was placed in this incongruous setting, Todd hunted for the nearest electrical outlet to plug it in. "Got to keep it working until the reading's taken," he muttered. "It's still under warranty."

Todd was no penman; he knew he could never imitate Grace's neat, educated handwriting. "I could never make it with the books," he once said of his schooldays. So he offered his young friends a deal. It wasn't stealing, he pointed out; the checks had been paid for by Grace, and she owed him the money. So if they would just sign her name and help him to cash them, he would divide the proceeds. Half-convinced, they accepted the offer, and a small cash flow was restored. But Layne Jackson, becoming more curious than ever about the strange visitor, phoned a freezer manufacturer one day to see how long the gadget inside the freezer had to be working before they could discover whether it was leaking. The man she spoke to did not seem to know what she was talking about. Things were becoming still more peculiar.

Mrs. Filman in Burlington became worried. She had not heard a word from Grace, David had borrowed quite a lot of money from her without any real security, and when she phoned his number, she found it was out of service. So on December 21 she made the journey to Don Mills and went to the apartment building at 1 Deauville Lane. There the superintendent told her the Todds were no longer tenants in the building. But Mrs. Filman knew that Grace's office was only a few minutes away, so she continued her inquiries there. Her alarm began to increase when she learned that her daughter's disappearance had been a matter of concern to her colleagues since August 17; what had since made the matter still more inexplicable was that Grace must be fully aware she would have money due to her if she left the company, but they had received no claim. She heard also of the efforts Ralph Pettyjohn had made to report Grace Todd's absence to the police, and how they had not known where they could get in touch with the family.

So just four days before Christmas, Mrs. Filman's report allowed Grace Todd to be finally entered officially as a missing person. It is probably a difficult season of the year to pursue inquiries of this nature, particularly when the missing person has not been seen for more than four months; it may be that the official view was that the mother and the employers were exaggerating the possibility of violence, or it may be the thought was entertained that if violence had occurred, there was no special urgency at so late a date. The building superintendent was not able to add much to what he had already told Mrs. Filman; he understood David Todd might have moved temporarily into one of the many townhouse units on Vendome Place, but was unable to say which or whether he was still there. Not much progress.

No information exists about how Christmas and the New Year holidays were spent at Mrs. Cassidy's townhouse unit.

Probably more merrily than by Grace's mother in Burlington and her sister in London. Mrs. Cassidy started to become annoyed with her self-invited lodger, however, when he showed no sign of preparing for departure in the first week of January. By January 11, a Wednesday, she reached the point of firmly demanding how soon he would be able to move out. "Just a couple of days," he told her. And then, since he always had the habit of adding a strange embellishment to a lie, he told her he was planning to go to Jamaica with two girls he had met.

Perhaps because the atmosphere had become so unfriendly, Todd went to bed early that night. Mrs. Cassidy went out. John Moore was over as usual, so he, Cathy, Charles and Layne settled down to watch television. After a while, they became bored. None of them knew who suggested it first; the idea was probably lurking at the back of all their minds. This was a wonderful opportunity, and possibly the last they would get if David Todd really was going to move out, to find what really was inside that mysterious freezer.

Later, it was hard for them to express what their real expectations were. The joke answer naturally was a body, or a head, or parts of a body: that was the kind of response invited by David's secrecy and annoyance when anybody fiddled with the lid. If someone like Vincent Price reacted that way in a horror movie, sure, that is what they would be expecting. But David Todd? It was fun to imagine, but the little guy couldn't be taken seriously as a wife-killer. He had something in there he didn't want anyone to see (girdles, whips, porno movies or maybe a dog he had run over?), but it would probably be a letdown. On the other hand . . .

When its lid was opened, the Continental SuperFreeze seemed to be offering the anti-climax they had expected. The lefthand basket contained half a gallon of ice cream, nine packages of frozen fish and what appeared to be a shriveled orange. The center basket held three turkey pies, some ice cubes, an opened packet of wieners, an opened packet of green peas, a loaf of bread and a package of bacon. The righthand basket offered a pint carton of ice cream, and unopened packages of green peas and carrots.

But lower down there appeared to be something else. When the baskets were shifted, they had their first sight of Grace Todd, dressed in a halter top and shorts, bent double and rigidly frozen. Startling in mid-January, her limbs carried the deep suntan of her Jamaican holiday. In the back of her head was a bullet wound.

Of course they called the police. When the car pulled up a few minutes later, David Todd was only half awake, sitting down with his head near his knees, but he gave the officers a wan smile. "Thank heaven you've come," he said. "I'm so glad it's over at last."

If the teenagers never knew exactly what to make of Todd, they cannot be blamed. The psychologists and psychiatrists who examined him over the next few weeks were equally unsure of what had really happened, or just when. As close as it can be placed, however, it was on the morning of Wednesday, August 4, Grace Todd's thirty-second birthday, the day the Todds had fixed to go camping, that the quarrel started in their living room. Todd did not remember what it was about. He only remembered that he was cleaning his Cooey rifle at the time, that Grace was lying on the settee and that she had told him their camping trip was off. He had asked her what she intended doing instead. She replied, he said, that after she had had an hour's sleep, she was going to get dressed, and that then she was going to pack, and that then she was going to walk out of the door and never come back. And he had been so shocked that the gun had gone off, although he had not thought it was loaded, and that the bullet had struck her in the forehead.

Todd's insistence that the bullet had entered the forehead, despite the clear evidence of a single bullet wound in the back of the head, is odd. An apparently pointless lie. The probability grew, in the minds of the doctors, that his belief in his account of his wife's death was complete. So, too, may have been his impression of her once visiting him after the shooting. His eyes moistened at any mention of her name; he always spoke of her adoringly.

In his weak little voice, he described the jealousy he had felt. "It got to the point I was watching everybody. Even my brother-in-law and my own brothers. I felt so much tension I sometimes wanted to scream." *But, O! what damned minutes tells he o'er, who dotes, yet doubts; suspects, yet strongly loves!* That described Othello. The psychiatrists believed the words could apply equally to David Todd. Both suffered from what, in the jargon of twentieth-century medicine, could be labeled as conjugal paranoia. But nobody could say, beyond reasonable doubt, whether he had intended to shoot his wife.

Found guilty on a charge of manslaughter on May 30, 1972, he was accordingly sentenced by Mr. Justice W. D. Parker to imprisonment for ten years. He was also prohibited from carrying firearms for a period of five years following his release, although it may be wondered if David Todd, either at fifty-two or sixty-two, would be someone much more trustworthy in the handling of firearms than he was at thirty-seven.

Time brings changes. Grace Todd's employers, the North American Life and Casualty Company (not to be confused, though it often was, with the North American Life Assurance Company), is at the same address but has become the Mony Life Insurance Company of Canada. Her evening haunt, the Mississippi Belle, has undergone extensive alteration to become the Latin Quarter. And the Continental SuperFreeze 507 that was her tomb for six months is now an exhibit in the museum on an upper floor of Metro Police Headquarters on Jarvis Street, Toronto.

Unaltered, though, is the uncertain question of the circumstances justifying an invasion of privacy in the public interest. In the Todd case, it was inevitable that the body would be discovered sooner or later. But it is disconcerting to reflect that if the curiosity of four teenagers had not overcome

their respect for adult privacy, it might have been considerably later. And if a less simple-minded means of concealment had been adopted, perhaps not at all.

Which, in turn, leads to the thought that perhaps David
Todd came to see the Continental SuperFreeze 507 not so
much as a hiding place but a secret shrine.

The Nestlings

Healthy young children are active, inquisitive and heedless. In consequence, they vanish from time to time, although seldom for long.

Every parent knows this, but the subconscious dread of an unnamable disaster only awaits the right moment to grip the heart and panic the mind. The age-old bogeys: a serious, perhaps fatal accident; abduction, sexual assault or murder; permanent disappearance, unexplained for many anxious weeks, if not forever.

Accidents undeniably do happen. Too frequently, even if not as often as imagination suggests. Sometimes currents and tides work in ways that result in an accidental death by drowning becoming a disappearance; in remote regions, foliage growth, rockfalls and deep snow can do the same.

Disappearances of young children by abduction involving force and assault are much rarer. The records seem to indicate that cases of that kind may be fewer today than thirty years ago, although there are no precise figures to verify this.

If this is so, the decrease has probably been exceeded by the number of quasi-domestic abductions in which one separated parent succeeds in removing his or her child from the custody of the other. These forays, which do not always violate criminal law, are a sociological phenomenon of the times, but since violence is seldom involved and the child's physical well-being is not endangered, these cases have not been made a part of this study.

On the other hand, even if there are fewer disappearances nowadays in which criminal assault can be proved or reasonably assumed, they continue to occur and will probably always be among the most distressing and most difficult challenges police forces must be prepared to tackle. They are frequently complicated by a defenseless victim offering no reason for the usual motives of hatred, revenge or greed; an unknown killer, probably unconnected to the victim, possibly a drifter with no local record; the lack of any productive clues or reliable evidence, and a time and place of abduction that is frequently unknown.

In the large majority of cases, the unlucky child is a female, but there are male victims, too. Separately, each of these disappearances is grim, disturbing and touchingly pathetic. Collectively, these cases take on a depressing sameness; one case begins to merge into the others. All that differs is whether or not the child's fate is eventually known, and whether or not an arrest was made and a conviction obtained. Even this, as will be seen, does not necessarily tell the whole story.

Most cases open in much the same way. A child fails to return at the expected time. At first, more irritation than concern, particularly if this has happened often before. A look from the window offers no sight of the child; perhaps a step outside into the backyard or out the front door will do better. Later comes the first stirring of the subconscious dread, and the visit to the homes of nearby parents of the child's friends, then phone calls further afield. In tightly knit communities, a volunteer search party is usually under way some time before it is thought necessary to ask for official help . . . which is sometimes a pity.

In 1967, in a case so typical of the period that it does not need specific identification, the search started by neighbors for a missing ten-year-old girl had been in progress for an hour before someone, realizing it would soon be dark that spring evening, thought to call the police at six-thirty.

The girl had left the school yard, less than a quarter mile from her home, at about four-fifteen. A witness was found who knew the girl by sight, and had seen her a little after that time entering a small dark station wagon, probably European, driven by a bespectacled middle-aged man. A seven-year-old school friend had seen the car. Three adults, driving west, had seen the car going east with a small figure seated beside the driver.

Later that evening detectives extended the search. It continued until late that night, and was resumed for the next eight days with volunteers pouring in from other localities and even other provinces in response to the feverish national coverage the media were providing. The police interviewed hundreds of European car owners, alibis were checked, conflicting reports compared and tested and so-called deviate files and recent discharges from mental institutions were searched, name by name. Half a year later, 188 out of an original total of 624 possible suspects were still the subjects of active investigation. But the nearest to a tangible clue was one small running shoe, which was found on the roadside about twenty miles away on the second day of the search. It appeared to be the girl's, but even that was without definite proof.

Aroused public emotions, focused on a mysterious human drama, can become hysterical and irresponsible, sometimes ugly. In most juvenile disappearances researched for this book, it is clear that time had to be made for investigating many unfounded but widely believed rumors. In this case, stories were circulating that the child had been kidnapped by her real father, the mother's former husband, or lover. An alternative offered was that the girl was a foster child, now abducted by her real parents. If any of this had been true, the whole course of the investigation might be wrong. In fact, it was all baseless. The mother had had no lover, this was her only marriage and the child was its legitimate outcome.

Nothing further has ever been discovered, and the case is officially still open. Although, after a while, the parents no longer allowed themselves to be excited by vague reports that their child had been momentarily sighted in cities across Canada, the United States or South America.

Nobody can say whether that child could have been recovered if the police had been called earlier, nor if harm to the investigation was caused by the hordes of eager and well-meaning volunteer searchers. It is possible she was already dead before the search began.

A similar child disappearance occurred eight years later in Moncton, New Brunswick. A seven-year-old girl went out on her bicycle after supper one July evening in 1975 and failed to return. Again a volunteer search party was formed, and it was not until nearly midnight, after many hours had been spent vainly scouring the neighborhood, that the city police were notified.

A witness who knew the girl by sight reported having seen her standing near a street corner at nine forty-five in the evening, and her bicycle was later found on a nearby lawn. A man who did not know her had a recollection of seeing a small, fair-haired girl who matched her description entering a small car somewhat later in the same locality. The car was described as dark green, possibly a Datsun, but nobody else seemed to have observed the incident.

An intensive local search went on through the night, and by the next day police forces across Canada were alerted to the girl's disappearance. Volunteer search parties continued in New Brunswick throughout the summer. No clues were found, and the case remains open.

On the first day of the girl's disappearance, the Moncton City Police issued a statement stressing the importance of prompt notification of a missing child, and their readiness to respond to any cause for concern. "Anxious parents should never feel they're bothering the police," their spokesman said.

No doubt in both these cases the neighborly support was so overwhelming from the moment the first agitated inquiry was made that everyone was sure the missing child must soon be found without official help. Neighbors, as they say, are there to help each other. Furthermore, until official help has been enlisted, the pain of recognizing that the child's life may really be endangered can be postponed.

Parents may often have other reasons to hesitate before asking police assistance, of course. There is a dread of disclosing family matters. They are felt to be nobody else's business, and are liable to be misinterpreted or met with public disapproval.

An early lesson a police officer learns about all missing-person investigations, especially missing children, is that the full facts are seldom voluntarily offered. The picture presented tends to be of a child always well behaved, punctual and obedient, deeply attached to always amicable parents and happy at school. The disappearance of such a child could only be accountable by unreported accident or foul play. The officer, aware that the odds are much more heavily in favor of forgetfulness, resentment or guilt about a minor transgression, obviously has questions to ask. Some policemen are probably better than others at this. It is far from easy to convey sympathy, skepticism and reassurance simultaneously. Without some further coaxing, there would be nothing learned about recently failed school tests, shoplifting escapades or possibly unduly severe punishments at school or at home. Nothing may be said about parental conflicts, although it may later emerge that one is a reluctant step-parent, or about frequent home arguments, or an impending break-up, or alcoholic problems in the home.

One or another of these factors usually plays a part in runaway disappearances, and however distressing these may be to the parents, runaways below teenage normally return sheepishly the same night or the following day, or are found promptly enough if sufficient confidence and trust has been established with the parents by the police officer.

One exception may be twelve-year-old Bobby Brown, who disappeared one Saturday evening in August 1968 from somewhere around Pefferlaw on Lake Simcoe, where his mother worked as the cook during the season at a religious summer camp. She was frank with the police; he was "not an easy boy to manage"; he was a handful at school and at home.

He was quite a small boy, only four foot six, and compactly built. A snapshot shows a fair, freckled face, dark blond hair, and a wide, confident grin. Sexuality was stirring in his blood; he had found a local date of his own age by the name of Toni, a ward of the Children's Aid Society.

The night before he disappeared, a Friday, Bobby had taken Toni to a carnival sponsored by the local Lions' Club and, having arrived home after midnight, had been grounded for the weekend. Someone saw him in front of a restaurant a few miles away on Georgia Beach at five-thirty the next afternoon. Nobody who knew him said that they had seen him since. Toni seemed genuinely distressed and denied hearing him speak of running away.

With a religious camp as his required daytime center of activity through that long summer, with two considerably younger brothers for playmates and a ten-month-old sister he had to baby-sit when his mother was otherwise engaged, Bobby fits the classic profile of the twelve-year-old runaway perfectly—except that he did not return, as others do, and was never heard of again.

However likely the runaway explanation may seem, the possibility of a more sinister explanation of a disappearance can never be disregarded. Dragging was conducted on the lake, scuba divers went down and helicopters took part in a widespread search. All without results. As the absence continued, vagrants were questioned and "deviate files" were worked over. Still nothing.

More than three weeks after Bobby's disappearance, a boy answering his description bought a Grey Coach ticket in Barrie to take him to Simcoe, where he said he was going to find work harvesting tobacco, but extensive inquiries in Simcoe failed to find the young traveler. Whether it was Bobby, whether he eluded the painstaking inquirers in the tobacco fields or whether he bought the ticket to provide a false scent is all anybody's guess. A snapshot of Bobby looking tough and happy in his football helmet conveys an impression that he is a born survivor.

It bears repetition for the anxious: most small children reported to be missing are home, safe and sound, within hours. False alarm though it may prove, a call to the police reduces the chance of a missing child being missing for longer. The smaller and more defenseless the child, the sooner a search will be organized and, unless the child is in hiding or has met with unusual misfortune, the sooner the worry will be ended.

Thousands of missing children are quickly found in this way by police forces across Canada every year, although reports of these minor victories seldom receive media attention. This chapter deals mainly with the exceptions; to disregard the victories is to see the failures in a false perspective.

Most searches are soon productive because they are based on a knowledge of the area and its particular dangers together with whatever has been learned of the child's usual activities, favorite local attractions and meeting places, and present state of mind. Although other police units will also be alerted, the first concentrated search will naturally focus on locations that seem to be likeliest. If the first day's search is unrewarded, it will be renewed the next day and broadened. If still unsuccessful, the process will have to be continued.

Nobody will want to say so openly, but there is an inner recognition that when a search begins with "probables," and proceeds to "just possibles," it is difficult to decide which direction is best after the "not impossible" solutions have been tried. With each day that goes by, the expectation of finding the child alive becomes less. If the mystery is ever solved, it will probably be by chance, and offer an unhappy answer.

A five-day search began on July 26, 1974, for four-year-old Cynthia "Cindy" Williams after she disappeared from outside the large Hamilton apartment building where she lived. She had gone down to play with another child after lunch, and another tenant saw her at the back of the building alone at two o'clock. Cindy was a likable child with many young friends in the building, but being scared of traffic, would never cross the busy street by herself. Accordingly, when she had not returned as usual to her fourth-floor apartment at four o'clock, and inquiries at other apartments gave no enlightenment, her mother called the police at four-thirty. Everything, in fact, done by the book.

Several city blocks and a nearby conservation area were combed in the prolonged search, but all the time Cindy's body lay in a shallow grave in a secluded and uncultivated field about four and a half miles away where it remained undiscovered for eight months. Undiscovered, but not altogether undisturbed by wild animals since some of the bones of the childish skeleton were never found, and by the end of April a small portion of the skull was visible under a cluster of hawthorn bushes. It might have gone unnoticed for much longer if it had not aroused the curiosity of a naturalist hunting for moss specimens.

Cindy's mother had insisted on her having regular dental checkups; it was only as a consequence of this that a positive identification of the skull was possible. (Dianne Williams stands out from the gray official depositions as an unusually loving and level-headed mother as well as a free-spirited young woman.) The girl's blue shorts and top, like her white underpants, pulled inside out, were buried in the same grave, leaving little doubt what had happened, but by that time the recovered evidence was insufficient to allow the cause of death to be determined.

At this point the Cindy Williams case resembles so many other sad, sordid discoveries, apparently destined to remain complete mysteries, that it hardly seems worth singling out. Its point of interest, however, is that fairly strong reasons exist to believe that the agent of her death is in custody as a result of a different, but not dissimilar, offense; that other serious charges with more compelling evidence are outstanding;

and that the individual will remain in custody, or under the strictest supervision, indefinitely.

The suspect has given statements that could be considered (although technically they are not) a series of confessions. Rambling, disjointed and sometimes contradictory, unmistakably the product of a disturbed mind, they furnish no more certainty in themselves than the scores of other "confessions" police, prison and other institutional officers are accustomed to receiving. (In the absence of corroboration, a confession of guilt carries no greater certainty than a protestation of innocence. Irrational guilt and gruesome fantasies are not uncommon. Neither is the wish to attract attention or create a mischievous diversion.)

The suspect in this instance, however, has a record of documented sex offenses from teenage years, incidents connected with several of the assaults described match with undisclosed evidence, and credibility has been added by other testimony that helps to establish a link to the Cindy Williams case. Some of the statements were made in circumstances that would debar them from use in court. That need is unlikely to arise.

Questions of civil rights, rules of evidence and the legal definition of insanity are all clearly relevant to this issue. The police are required to carry out the law as it stands, and the result is that the number of unapprehended child-killers will always be less than the official records indicate.

In this particular case, the individual seems to resemble the wretched monster who haunts popular imagination, intent on both sexual violation and the infliction of death on a young child. Forensic psychiatrists, however, state that this type, devoid of affect and conscience, does not represent the majority of child-killers. Such deaths are more usually unpremeditated, the consequence of panic, guilt or shame, or even accidental: the work of badly disturbed individuals who have acted out an uncontrollable fantasy. While psychological patterns may recur, child-killers vary greatly in their outward appearances. The police can take nothing for granted. It may, for example,

seem unnecessarily cautious to employ terms neutral enough
to imply that the individual may not always be male.

In a celebrated English case in which the strangled body
of a small girl was apparently sexually assaulted, the killer
proved to be a middle-aged woman who had murdered the
child from spite, and mutilated the body with a screwdriver
to disguise her guilt. There have been other cases of one or
both parents reporting a child to be missing after disposing of
the body.

Most frequently the fact is child-killers are not related to,
or even acquainted with, the child. They are themselves often
children of long-parted parents, forced to find some kind of
independence at an early age, despite—or just as likely, because of—crippling personality disorders already in evidence.
By a grim irony, individuals who become the agents of a
child's disappearance may be missing persons themselves in a
sense, although never reported as such. With spotty records of
casual employment and imprisonment, their whereabouts only
become known to their relatives when some new disaster envelopes them. The knowledge is something the relatives are
likely to try to forget as soon as possible; even if a wish to
help existed, it probably could not be fulfilled.

With few exceptions, the prospects of the individual
proving responsive to treatment, and attaining an acceptable
degree of normality, unfortunately lie, at the present stage of
medical science, on the gloomy side of uncertainty. Uncontrollable impulses may first be manifested in puberty or adolescence. They sometimes diminish naturally after middle age,
but suspects cannot be restricted to any specific age group.

Eight-year-old Lisa Ann Kowalski, a pretty little girl just
fifty inches tall, nicely built with fair complexion, good teeth,
short brown hair and blue eyes, must have looked rather like
Little Red Riding Hood on that cold January day in 1976.
There was snow on the ground, and she was wearing black
boots, a red woollen toque and a full-length red and blue coat
and hood with fur trim when she left her home in a north-
western Toronto suburb at noon.

She had left early to do some shopping for her mother in the local mall and call back home with her purchases before going on to school. After she left, however, her mother noticed that she had forgotten the twenty-dollar bill she had been supposed to take. Since the child did not return to collect it, her mother assumed she had made the discovery too late to turn back, and had decided to go straight to school.

After Lisa failed to return at the usual time, it occurred to her mother that Lisa, not knowing she had left the money behind, might be afraid of being blamed for losing it somewhere on the street. As time dragged by, and none of her inquiries brought news of her daughter, she became increasingly worried and called the police at seven o'clock. To the police, the mother's theory for her daughter's absence sounded quite likely; a prompt and thorough search might soon be fruitful.

It was not. It continued without success all night and for many days after. Teams from four police divisions took part and directed the efforts of thousands of volunteers, including many members of snowmobile trail clubs. After ten days of intensive search, defeat had to be acknowledged.

Eighteen weeks after Lisa disappeared spring brought warmer weather. The maintenance superintendent of a row of townhouses close to Lisa's home received a complaint from one of the tenants about an odor filling her home. It did not take him long to locate its source, and to put in a frantic call to the police. Using his master key, he had entered a garage adjoining the house which had been overcome by the odor. The garage was used by its owner only for storage. There he had found a foul-smelling green garbage bag stuffed in an otherwise empty broken crate on a pile of other crates and cartons. One glimpse inside the bag revealed the decomposing remains of a small girl.

The same afternoon, the police had arrested the owner's seventeen-year-old son half an hour after his father, urgently summoned by his mother, had hurried home from his office. Lisa's death, acknowledged by the youth in a state of numbed shock, had been the sequel to his inviting her into the house on that cold January day.

He had been in the garden, had seen her passing in the rear lane and acted on impulse. He had seen her before in the neighborhood as she had probably seen him, but they had never spoken. Now, because nobody else was at home, he invited her in. Possibly because it was not yet time for her to be in school and this offered a chance to get warm, or out of friendliness, or just out of curiosity, she had accepted.

That was as much as the youth could bring himself to tell. A search of his room had produced clear evidence that he was undergoing the disturbing experiences of adolescence in lonely sexual fantasies. Hidden in a closet had been found a padded, life-size doll encrusted with semen, obviously his frequent source of relief. No clear account was obtained by the police, or later by psychiatrists, of what had ensued that January afternoon. All that could be established was that Lisa Kowalski had been strangled, and that before his mother had returned, the youth had hidden her body, bundled into the garbage bag, in the then ice-cold garage.

One unexpected discovery was made at the autopsy. Lisa Kowalski had unquestionably died a virgin, and no evidence was found of sexual molestation. There can be little doubt that the purpose for which she had been persuaded into the house was far from innocent. A possible explanation could have been her would-be raper's inability to perform, faced for the first time with a real body.

The Young Gentlemen
of the Lake

She was born in the east end of Toronto and christened Minnie Olive Fenn. When she was fifteen, in 1922, she found work locally as a sewing machine operator and continued steadily at this rather monotonous trade through the Depression and the Second World War.

At twenty-seven, she had met Lorne Ford, one year younger than herself. Their courtship advanced slowly since he was going through the painful process of a divorce separating him from a son and daughter; moreover, regular jobs were scarce in those depression years. Even after their marriage on her twenty-ninth birthday on May 23, 1936, their circumstances made it necessary for them to postpone any thought of a family of their own.

The war was instrumental in transforming their lives. Lorne had been among the first to enlist, and when he was discharged with the rank of captain from the Royal Canadian Army Service Corps in 1945, he possessed a thorough knowledge of automotive engineering, vehicle maintenance and administration procedure. He promptly enrolled in a training course offered by a major oil company, and six months later was able to open a well-located service station in Willowdale, a growingly prosperous suburb to the north of Toronto.

It had also seemed possible to consider parenthood again.

High time, in fact, since Minnie was now near thirty-nine. To their delight, a baby boy who would be baptized as Wayne Lorne Ford was born on June 9, 1946.

Lorne Ford's career in those early post-war years was almost a textbook example of the success rewarding diligence and good citizenship. He worked untiringly at his business, and it prospered. He was prominent in fraternal societies, he learned to play a fair game of golf and became known as a keen angler and hunter, as well as a devoted family man. In 1951 the Ford family moved from their small house in east Toronto to one on Stuart Crescent nearer Lorne's service station in Willowdale; by 1953 they had bought a summer cottage on Lake Couchiching, little more than an hour's drive north; and in 1956 they had moved their residence to a larger Willowdale home at 21 Kingsdale Avenue, on the slightly more fashionable eastern side of Yonge Street.

They took summer vacations at the cottage, and other vacations in Florida, California and Mexico. In 1958, since Minnie was afraid of flying, Lorne flew with his twelve-year-old son as his companion for a trip to Europe, and in 1959 the family bought a new Cadillac. Within the next two years, Lorne began buying property in Florida. He had arrived.

Only one blemish could have marred his contentment. He may have had a faint realization that he had sired a monster.

Even before the family moved to Willowdale, little Wayne's self-confidence and willfulness were ceasing to be cute. As he grew older and larger, there were occasions when his strong-willed selfishness and hot temper worried his parents, and as his weight and size began reaching the point where they were losing the power of physical domination, they were sometimes a little frightened. On the other hand, they told themselves, the lad was undoubtedly bright, and everybody was talking of the need to adjust to a new generation and new ways of behavior.

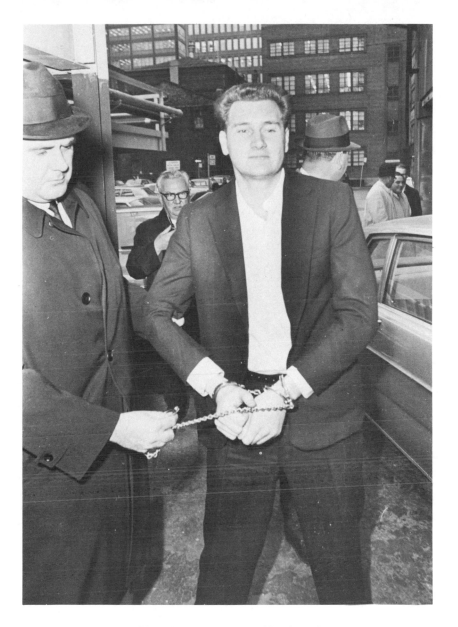

Wayne Ford. Only one blemish may have marred his father's contentment. He may have had a faint realization that he had sired a monster. ("The Young Gentlemen of the Lake") Copyright, reproduced by kind permission of The Globe and Mail, *Toronto*

Opposite page: "The Casselman Floater"; police artist's reconstruction. ("Remains in Doubt") Courtesy of the Ontario Provincial Police

Bottom: The unusual dentures she was wearing. ("Remains in Doubt") Courtesy of the Ontario Provincial Police

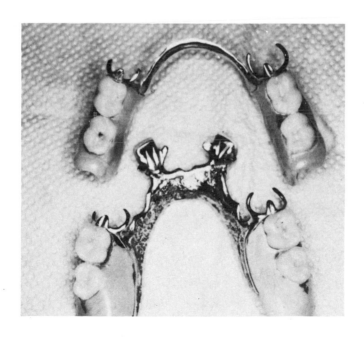

Mary Kathleen Misener in 1981—member of a gambling club known as The Circle. ("Remains in Doubt") Copyright, Canapress Photo

Whether events would have followed a very different course if they had summoned the courage to bundle young Wayne off for psychotherapy is debatable; expert opinion given some years later in court confirmed that Wayne Ford possessed what is described as a psychopathic or sociopathic personality, a condition for which the prospects of wholly successful treatment are never optimistic. Its origin is obscure; nobody is sure why such personalities occur, only that they do, sometimes in families where other children show no similar tendencies. The upbringing Wayne Ford received, however, as the over-indulged and inconsistently disciplined only child of middle-aged parents enjoying their first taste of affluence, made matters worse.

Lorne was at least aware that his son's increasing waywardness was upsetting his wife. It had, in fact, done something to alienate her from her own relations who were loud in their criticism of the boy's rudeness and disobedience, and generous with suggestions for appropriate correctional training; it was the main reason she saw them less often. But Lorne, possibly with memories of the two children of his first marriage who were lost to him, told Minnie he could not bring himself to treat Wayne with real severity "in case he lost the boy's love."

To distract himself from this unhappy domestic situation, Lorne Ford threw himself even more vigorously into his lodge meetings, his hunt club outings, his business luncheons and, above all, his commercial enterprises. Perhaps as a result, he had to consult his doctor in 1961 about some unusual pains he had started to experience.

The doctor's diagnosis was serious; the condition of Lorne's heart meant that he must learn to take things much more easily. This was the kind of situation Lorne could handle; it offered a logical solution. Before the year was out, the service station had been sold to Gordon Sanford, his second-in-command for so long he had become a family friend. Shortly after he drove south with Minnie and Wayne, not for their normal short vacation, but for the purpose of deciding on which of the five properties he had purchased in Florida they would build their retirement home.

While still en route, Lorne had a minor heart attack. He felt better in the morning, but the next day he suffered a more severe attack in the motel and died in the hospital to which he had been rushed by ambulance. Somehow Minnie managed to go through the procedure of arranging for the body to be returned to Willowdale for burial, and of organizing the return journey for Wayne and herself. But her heart must have been full of foreboding for the future.

It would be misleading to imagine Minnie Ford at this stage as the traditionally frail and retiring widow, shy of dealing with the outside world. She had been putting on some weight since the war, but she was still quite active, looking younger than her fifty-five years; her brown hair was only beginning to be flecked with gray, and she seldom troubled to wear her glasses. Although she was not the easy social mixer her husband had become, she had her own circle of friends and enjoyed driving the Cadillac and an evening's bowling. As the main beneficiary of Lorne's $80,000 estate ($15,000 was set aside as a trust for Wayne, primarily for the purpose of higher education), she engaged wisely in local real estate investment. If it had not been for the ever-present problem of her son, she was a woman who could have brought her widowhood under reasonable control.

Of the several unsuccessful ways of handling a son of Wayne's temperament, she had adopted the one bound to be most exhausting for herself and the likeliest to lead to a disastrous climax: she tried to shout him down. Wayne was now a 180-pound sixteen year old, and at six feet towered seven inches above her; sometimes he simply disregarded her presence, sometimes he screamed back more loudly and gesticulated more violently.

In other respects, Minnie Ford could be regarded as a conventionally good mother. She gave him occasional use of the Cadillac, and Wayne complained it was too infrequent; she provided him with a reasonable allowance, and he grumbled at its inadequacy; she prepared him good meals he frequently refused to eat; she intervened on his behalf when his high school principal threatened suspension if he persisted in wearing outlandish clothing in class, and Wayne cursed her for trying to make him a conformist.

When his use of the Cadillac was curtailed after he had had his first accident, he bought a 1949 Ford without her knowledge; when this too was involved in a crash, she had to pay his fifty-dollar fine. Another fine of twenty-five dollars had to be paid when Wayne was charged with carrying a concealed weapon—a hunting knife. Less than a month after the first anniversary of his father's death, Wayne involved the Cadillac in another serious smash and a repair charge of $1,087. To the trade friend who carried out the work and to her friends as well, Minnie Ford vowed that her son would never be allowed to drive the car again. But discussion of the matter with Wayne took the form of her usual outraged screaming.

On May 16, 1963, the Thursday before the Victoria Day weekend, the Cadillac once more stood in the driveway of 21 Kingsdale Avenue, restored to immaculate glossiness. Aware that the sanctions his mother imposed in anger were not always enforced, Wayne apparently asked for the use of the car for a weekend at the cottage. As it happened, this was a singularly inauspicious time for such a request. Other considerations apart, Minnie was probably just about to phone her elder sister who lived nearby in Etobicoke to confirm the arrangement they had previously discussed to take a drive down to the Niagara Peninsula to admire the blossoms. But her sister received no call from Minnie that Thursday or ever again.

It was about eight in the evening of the following Wednesday that one of Minnie's oldest friends called her for a chat. Her friendship with Lorne and Minnie went back over thirty-five years, and she was a woman in whom Minnie confided. Wayne informed her simply that his mother was "out somewhere." Did that mean, the friend asked, that the Cadillac was back on the road? Perhaps suspecting that the question had not been asked quite innocently, Wayne could not resist the opportunity to inform her offhandedly that he had smashed it up again over the weekend. Then he hung up.

Wayne's taunt was true but rash. Recalling his mother's vow that he would never be allowed to drive the car again, her friend phoned back minutes later demanding to be told where his mother was. All he could tell her, Wayne said, was that she was staying at a friend's cottage for about a week; he did not know whose cottage or where it was. Dissatisfied, the friend then called Minnie's sister in Etobicoke, and heard of the proposed trip to Niagara, and the telephone call of confirmation the sister had been expecting but never received. Now thoroughly alarmed, she phoned Gordon Sanford, the Ford's family friend who operated the service station, and asked if he did not think the circumstances should be investigated.

Puzzled, Sanford drove round to the Ford house. Since lights were on in almost every room, he judged that Wayne was not alone. He kept watch for more than an hour, but nobody left. The next morning he related the whole story to Archibald Greenaway, Minnie Ford's own solicitor. Greenaway had no doubts on the proper action; he took Sanford with him to the Willowdale police station where the solicitor reported his client as a missing person.

Two detectives immediately made the first of what would be many visits over the next three years to the Ford home. Wayne let them in. He seemed to be alone, but a few minutes later another hulking long-haired youth sauntered into the room, apparently unaware of their arrival. Both detectives thought the visitor seemed dismayed by their presence—probably not an unusual teenage reaction to the law—and noticed his quick, wordless departure from the room.

Wayne explained that the youth they had just seen was his close friend Ron Walli, who had been one of his two companions over the past weekend, and who was staying with him for a few days. Ron, as a matter of fact, had been with him when he had last seen his mother, which had been at about half past nine on the previous Saturday morning. The detectives suggested it might be a good idea for Wayne and his friend Ron to take advantage of the facilities for having complete statements taken at the police station. Wayne at once agreed. Ron was called, and a little later they were both being led separately over their accounts of everything that had happened over the past six days. In all essential respects, their statements tallied.

As they told it, Minnie Ford had suggested that Wayne and two of his school friends should spend the Victoria Day weekend up at the Ford cottage on Lake Couchiching, and that to allow them to make an early start on the Saturday morning, Ron, whose home was in Downsview, some miles away, had slept at 21 Kingsdale Avenue, on Friday night. On Saturday morning, after making them breakfast, Wayne's mother had said she must spend a day or so with other unspecified friends; the boys should accordingly drive up to Lake Couchiching without her, but that she expected to join them on the Monday or Tuesday. They had gone ahead as she suggested, driving north after they had picked up a third youth, Larry Metcalfe, who lived locally.

Their weekend, as they recalled it, had been relatively uneventful except for one unfortunate incident; driving to a midnight dance in Orillia on the Sunday, Wayne had had an accident requiring the Cadillac to be taken to a body shop in that city, leaving them without transportation. Consequently, since Wayne's mother had not shown up at the cottage by Tuesday night, they had arranged for Ron Walli's father to drive up to the cottage on Wednesday to bring them back. Wayne's mother's own plans had been vague, and they had not been alarmed when she failed to arrive, but they really had no idea where she was now. Anyway, they had been getting along so badly, Wayne added, he would not be really surprised if she had decided to desert him.

Having taken statements from Wayne and Ron, the next step for the detectives was to interview the third boy, Larry Metcalfe. Larry proved to be only a fifteen-year-old and rather more conventional in appearance and dress than the other two, but he already resembled them in size. He provided his own account of the weekend, which offered no substantial contradiction to the statements the detectives already had. On the face of it, their stories were straightforward enough; the story of the car accident was obviously something that could be confirmed. Wayne's knowledge of his mother's movements was admittedly remarkably sketchy, but as the detectives were aware, older and younger generations confided less to each other, and if on occasions one might try, the other seldom listened with much interest.

For all that, there was something suspiciously pat about the boys' stories; as a matter for more immediate action, the detectives had noticed certain things that seemed to need further investigation at 21 Kingsdale Avenue. In consequence, Wayne Ford found himself in court again four days later, charged with possession of goods reported stolen from cottages near to the Ford cottage at the lake, and for possession of a sawed-off shot gun.

Unruffled, Wayne granted that the break-in was an incident he had omitted from his original statement. Otherwise he held to his story. In view of his age, he received a suspended sentence with a year's probation.

Soon after that a group of detectives and a biologist from the Centre of Forensic Science paid a visit to the Ford cottage on Lake Couchiching. They inspected the cottage and the lakeside, and interviewed some of the summer residents; they also carefully examined the wrecked Cadillac in the Orillia body shop where it was undergoing repairs, and spoke to the policemen who had interrogated the boys after Wayne had smashed it. There was much to arouse their suspicions, but nothing tangible enough to complete a case. One thing was certain, however; the weekend had been more eventful than the story the boys had told had indicated. Mildewing and still-damp clothing in the cottage suggested unreported high jinks in the lake, and the seven hundred extra miles clocked on the Cadillac's register in the three days after leaving the Willowdale body shop widened the field of possible speculation regarding Minnie Ford's disappearance.

It seemed impossible that one fifteen-year-old and two sixteen-year-old boys, questioned separately, would individually have the resolution to stick to their original statements indefinitely. But however often the detectives went over the same ground, they seemed to be unshakable. Wayne Ford even consented to take a polygraph test; the results were inconclusive. The detectives became as sure as the missing woman's friends had been from the outset that her son knew the explanation of her disappearance, but were unable to find it for themselves.

Diabolically, Wayne Ford complicated their task by making mock confessions with a leer to other teenagers who asked what had happened to his mother. Sometimes he said he had bricked her up behind a fireplace. Sometimes he said he had stuffed her down a well. He told one group he had cut her up in small pieces and dropped them in the lake. Another time he told a girl visitor the body was under the sofa she was sitting on. Someone asked him why he had killed his mother. "For her money. What else?" he answered straightfaced.

None of his mother's estate could be yet in his control, of course, but he soon found ways of selling the house furniture. He had dropped out from Earl Haig Collegiate, and needed extra funds to finance round-the-clock parties at 21 Kingsdale Avenue for all the other teenage dropouts in the area who liked to come. Most of them had had trouble with the law, but Wayne was king, as well as a lavish host. Beer and liquor were available at all times. So was indiscriminate sex. Some friends moved in permanently, others might stay overnight. Wayne, garishly dressed and ornamented, led the revels. At intervals, sure that his line was tapped, he would pick up the phone and yell "Stupid dumb coppers!" followed by a string of obscenities; it was a guaranteed mirth-provoker for his guests. If anyone was rash enough to oppose him on a point, he would growl, "I've killed once, and I'm ready to kill again."

One merry evening he proposed to some other youths that they should take turns in balancing a spool of thread on their heads down in the basement, and that they should see who could shoot it off with a .22 rifle. When nobody would risk it, the target was changed to a corncob bowl balanced on the end of a ruler gripped in the mouth, with hits being rewarded with a slug of blackberry brandy. Their marksmanship became erratic. One youth was shot in the foot and had to be taken to the hospital.

Wayne consequently made his next appearance in court on a charge of criminal negligence causing bodily harm. Although he was still on probation, a generous-minded magistrate accepted the assurance of Wayne's lawyer, George Brigden, that his client had since undergone a change of heart; another suspended sentence was imposed. (It is necessary to remember that this was the era of pop psychology, when "there were no bad children, only bad parents." Even Wayne's rumored boastings of having murdered his mother could support the opposite theory that she had run out on him. Rather than accept his mother's rejection, some said, he preferred to claim that it was he who had done away with her.)

His lawyer's hopes for Wayne's reformation proved unfounded. In March 1964, apparently homeless, he was found sleeping in the lobby of an apartment building and received a one-month sentence for vagrancy. On his eighteenth birthday, he and his old friend, Ron Walli, with whom he had been reliving old times breaking and entering lakeside cottages around Lake Couchiching, received twelve-month concurrent sentences on each of four charges of possession, and a three-month sentence, also concurrent, on a charge of willful damage.

He and Ron had not been out of prison long after serving this sentence when they went into partnership again. On September 27, 1965, they were both sentenced to two years imprisonment at the Burwash Industrial Prison Farm for stealing luggage from the lockers of a Willowdale apartment building on Yonge Street. Wayne by this time was a remarkable sight; he had grown to six feet and three inches, weighed two hundred pounds, and had had his face tattooed. When stripped he was more spectacular still; a large picture of Disney's Goofy covered one shoulder, his prison number was defiantly tattooed on his arm and two rosy-red lips were tattooed on his buttocks.

On May 17, 1966, he and another inmate escaped, but Wayne was hardly inconspicuous. He was recaptured three days later, sentenced to serve an extra six months and transferred to Kingston Penitentiary.

During the second week of October of the same year, a cottage dweller on Lake Couchiching noticed an object he took to be a discarded store mannequin lying near the shoreline, but did not investigate it closely. On the morning of October 16 someone else, taking a closer look, was horrified to find it was a decomposing human body, crouched up. The provincial police were called, the corpse was transferred to the provincial forensic pathologists in Toronto and the gruesome work of providing positive identification was begun.

The head was damaged and hairless; the face, which was skinless and eyeless, was unrecognizable; one hand was missing. Parts of the body, moreover, appeared to be encased in plaster; this later proved to be adipocere—fat drawn from the body by prolonged immersion, which had hardened externally. But the general condition of the corpse was consistent with immersion in lake water for something between two and four years: the sex, age and body structure all conformed with descriptions given of the missing woman: and after a detailed examination had been concluded, the pathologists had verified that these were Minnie Ford's remains.

A bigger problem was determination of the cause of death; not because of any lack of evidence, but because so many possibilities were open. The damage to the skull was extensive, but could have been caused in the water; marks around the throat might have been caused by strangulation. The likeliest cause, however, seemed to be a fairly slim pointed metallic spindle, about two inches long, embedded in one side of the skull. X-ray examination showed that a similar length of metal rod would be discovered inside the skull, although the skull was too damaged to provide certainty as to how it had entered.

Up at the lake, scuba divers and closed circuit TV cameras were used to search the lake bottom over the area between the Ford cottage and the point where the body had come ashore. This brought to light many portions of a plywood box and fragments of clothing, as well as a large pair of suede shoes and a leather wriststrap, both of the type known to have been worn by Wayne Ford, portions of a canvas kitbag stenciled RCASC and having the initial F inked on it, a cut-down baseball bat, and the corpse's missing hand.

With all this new evidence, the investigation into the disappearance of Minnie Ford could be moved back into top gear. Wayne and Ron Walli were now both twenty-year-olds, and Larry Metcalfe was nineteen. Wayne, interviewed at Kingston Penitentiary, had nothing further to say. Walli, interviewed at his demand in the presence of Wayne Ford's lawyer, George Brigden, adamantly refused to change his previous statement; he knew nothing whatever, he said, to explain the body that had been found.

Questioning of Larry Metcalfe began at eight-thirty on the morning of Wednesday, November 9. After five hours of denying all knowledge of how the body had come to be in the lake, he suddenly stood up and said he wanted to tell the truth. Following his revised statement, he was given the routine warning and charged with murder.

Learning of this, Walli had the sense to recognize he would be putting himself into even more danger than Metcalfe was now facing if he continued to hold out. So with a different lawyer to represent him, he in turn made a confession of his involvement. Since all three youths had been roaring drunk for much of that weekend, Walli's account was not identical with Metcalfe's, particularly in respect of the sequence of events; more remarkable, however, was the number of points on which the two separately given accounts agreed. Pieced together, a reasonably coherent outline emerges although, quite naturally, both Walli and Metcalfe were anxious to emphasize (and, according later to Wayne Ford's lawyers, over-emphasize) the extent to which they had been made reluctant participants in the gruesome proceedings.

It had all started, apparently, when Wayne's mother had refused to let him borrow the Cadillac on the Thursday before the Victoria Day weekend in 1963. Wayne had flown into a violent temper and his mother had screamed back at him. After they had yelled childish insults at each other for some time, Wayne lost all control of himself. He had hit his mother hard several times on the side of the head with his cut-down baseball bat. Then he tried to strangle her with his hands. After she had fallen to the floor, he began stabbing her in the head with an ice pick, which had finally broken off short after penetrating the bone.

Had a second ice pick—to account for the other pointed object found inside the skull—suffered the same fate? Perhaps, but Wayne apparently never said so; in fact, he later hotly denied it, making the fragment an unexplained, but unimportant, mystery. According to Walli, Wayne said that "he had hit her, and hit her, and found he couldn't stop." (Wayne's later story was to be that it was his mother who first attacked him with the ice pick, after he had slapped her face. He had then, he said, picked up the bat to defend himself. That was not what Walli remembered being told.)

When his mother lay still, he put a blue bag over her damaged and bleeding head, tying it round her neck. Then he covered the body with a sheet and, presumably after washing and changing, drove the Cadillac round to Earl Haig Collegiate to meet Ron Walli as he left that afternoon. Driving him back to Kingsdale Avenue, he told him what had happened, and demanded his help. Walli said Wayne kept fingering a loaded .38 revolver lying on the floorboard, and made it clear he was not in the mood for argument. When Wayne removed the sheet to show him the body, Walli said, he had promptly vomited in the kitchen sink. Then, at Wayne's prompting, he had helped him drag the body downstairs to the basement, leaving smears of blood along the way. Between them, they then folded the body into a hinged plywood box some three feet wide by two feet deep. The sheet, a mat and other items were put in to avoid further staining, and the lid was loosely secured with a length of plastic hosing. Then, after they had made plans for the next day, Walli had gone home for supper. It was only five-thirty.

Almost incredibly, both youths attended school the next morning, Wayne in the Cadillac. At midday, after picking up clothes for the weekend from Walli's home, they got down to the serious business of scrubbing, scraping and repainting to remove the bloodstains from the kitchen, the stairs and the basement at 21 Kingsdale Avenue. That done, they started drinking. A few hours later they went to a drive-in movie. Later that night they returned to the house, loaded the box into the trunk of the Cadillac and set off for the cottage. There Wayne collected some digging tools before setting off again down a dirt road, and at what seemed to be a suitable spot, told Walli to help dig a grave.

It was a hopeless endeavor. For one thing, the ground was too hard for inexperienced diggers; for another, Walli was in no condition to help, having been vomiting drunkenly for much of the journey. They accordingly returned to the cottage, carried the box and the tools into the garage, locked the door and drove back to Willowdale, arriving in the early hours of Saturday morning.

They had decided they needed another companion. Metcalfe was not their first choice, but after they had been cruising around for some time finding that most of their friends were either already away or had other holiday plans, the fifteen-year-old youth seemed the likeliest prospect. Presumably at that point they required a third youth who would later be able to say that the weekend had passed uneventfully except that Mrs. Ford, who Wayne and Walli had been expecting to arrive on Monday, never showed up; in that case, Wayne and Walli would have returned to the cottage later in the week to dispose of the body. If that was the original plan, it began to slip when they started drinking from the several cases of beer and six bottles of liquor they had also loaded in the car.

The three youths did not arrive at the lake until the late afternoon, having first attended a movie matinee. On arrival, they made a social round of teenagers at the other cottages, drinking freely wherever the opportunity arose, and it was then that, when asked whether Wayne's mother was up that weekend, the macabre jokes were first made about her murder and disposal. Wayne, the great kidder. Later that evening, the three took off for a beer store in Barrie to replenish their dwindling stocks, and returned to the cottage to continue the party. Walli, quite drunk, went outside, lost his way and spent the night sleeping on the floor of a neighboring cottage. After he had found his way back on Sunday morning, the three drove around wildly, adding some of those extra miles on the Cadillac's odometer that were to lead the police on many false trails.

Apparently, it was only after their return after dark that Wayne Ford made Metcalfe forcibly aware that he really had killed his mother; he was made to open the box to savor the now mephitic corpse. Any account of what followed becomes credible only by assuming that the enormity of this crime in relation to all their previous youthful transgressions, added to the exhilaration induced by hours of reckless driving in a high-powered car, the level of alcohol in their bloodstreams and their isolation from the adult world, combined to produce a state of complete unreality.

Just a few initial qualms. Walli rebelled when ordered to

use pliers to extract the broken ice pick from the corpse's skull. "No way," he muttered. "No way." Ford then handed him a heavy length of rail, telling him to smash the teeth from the corpse's mouth to hamper identification. Afraid to show reluctance, Walli afterwards claimed, he left the room to obey but returned after only closing the lid, and nodded when Ford demanded whether he had done the job. Ford stared hard at him, and growled, "You fucking better had."

That was the prologue; then the first act of the horror show moved forward, with breaks for hysterical giggling. For example, there was the choice of Wayne's childhood play wagon as the hearse to convey the makeshift coffin to its improvised funeral barge, the old boat at the dock. For example, there was a ludicrous attempt to tie a stolen anchor around the corpse's neck to provide extra weight, and the decision to tie it, banglelike, to the hand that later became detached. For example, the box was found to be wedged in the stern of the boat after they had rowed a thousand feet from the shore, and tried to offload it.

Their combined pushing succeeded in dislodging not just the box but the entire transom of the decrepit boat. Into the lake went the three young gentlemen as the boat slowly turned turtle. For a climax, while they clung to the upturned wreckage, the frail coffin bobbed gently to the surface and a crimson circle enlarged around them.

None of them was sure of being able to swim the distance, so finally Ford ordered Walli to cast off. Somehow Walli succeeded, chopped a neighbor's boat free from its moorings and returned to rescue them. In the meantime, Ford, still brandishing aloft a loaded revolver, had reconsigned his mother to the deep by leaning all his weight onto the plywood box until enough water had entered. Back on shore, they were frenzied with excitement. So into dry clothes, and off to the midnight dance. On the way there or back, an impromptu drag race with other youths took place down Orillia's streets—and there, at a speed of a hundred miles an hour, the Cadillac spun out of control into a post, and its occupants, unharmed, were driven back to the cottage. (Little wonder if they sensed they were invulnerable.)

Sleeping late on Monday morning, they spent the afternoon disporting with local teenage girls. Later, hungry and adventurous, they broke into unoccupied lakeshore cottages for food and whatever took their fancy. On Tuesday, they hatched the story of the innocent weekend which they swore to uphold against all pressure from authority. A more immediate question also had to be faced—how to return home without a car. Someone must hitch a ride to arrange transportation for the others. Ford's first thought was to send the ever-obedient Walli; a closer look at his friend made him think otherwise. "He told me," Walli remembered, "that my hair was too long, and I looked too much of a mess for anybody to want to stop for me." So it was Larry who went, but not before being warned again to tell no one of the weekend's real happenings. Otherwise, Ron would get it from Wayne. And Larry had better remember he was now as much implicated as they were.

The first part of the horror show, lasting less than a week, was over. The second part, extending more than a thousand days, then began. The statements finally provided by Metcalfe and Walli could, indeed, have made them liable to prosecution as accessories after the fact. They were, however, needed as Crown witnesses to insure Wayne Ford's conviction on the charge of non-capital murder.

After a sensational trial, Ford was sentenced to life imprisonment on May 30, 1967. The sentence was upheld by the Ontario Court of Appeal six months later.

Remains in Doubt

The natural converse of a missing live person must be an unidentified dead body. Unidentified bodies are rarer than missing persons, and it seldom takes long to make at least a tentative identification by a comparison of the physical characteristics of the body with the detailed descriptions on record of people who have been reported missing around the period estimated by the pathologist to have elapsed since death. This, however, does not always solve the mystery of the disappearance.

A male body found floating in Quebec City Harbour in May 1976, just after the ice break-up, remained unidentified until the description was positively matched with that of a partner in a well-known travel agency on Toronto's Bay Street, missing since October of the previous year. There were no indications of violence, nor could any of his friends or relatives offer a reason for his visit to Quebec City without informing anyone of his intention. He was described as a quiet, unmarried man; nobody knew of private worries, and the agency's books were in perfect order. Identification of the body meant that one more missing person had been located, but a puzzle persists.

Positive identification inevitably takes longer if decomposition is advanced or when severe disfigurement or tissue

destruction has been sustained. In these cases, the exacting
process required for positive identification may sometimes
seem excessive until it is realized how easily an apparently
safe assumption can prove incorrect and how painful this
could be for a missing-person's family.

In some cases the remains may be relatively well preserved, but when they do not seem to fit the description of
any missing person on record, help has to be asked from the
public. This is the reason the drawer shelves in the refrig-
erated cabinets of the impressively hygienic morgue forming
part of the Forensic Pathology Division in Toronto will generally contain about eight bodies on which autopsies have already been conducted, but to which no identity can yet be assigned.

For the most part, they represent a transient population,
but there is one who seems likely to qualify as a semiper-
manent resident. Among the first to be received after the
building was opened in 1975 was a body entered on the records as Body Number 074. To those familiar with the case, it
is that of the Casselman floater.

Highway 417 crosses the Nation River just west of Casselman, around thirty-five miles from Ottawa in one direction
and from the Quebec border in the other. On the morning of
May 3, 1975, a body was seen floating face down in the river,
about a hundred yards from the bridge, naked except for a
blue shirtlike garment bundled about the neck and shoulders.
What looked to be some heavier material was wrapped
around the head.

Brought ashore by the police, the body proved to be that
of a young woman, and had obviously been in the water some
time. The wrists were laced together in front with a man's
necktie, and two other neckties had been used to secure the
ankles. The neckties at the ankles were nondescript. One was
blue and gray, the other, red and white; both unidentifiable.
The necktie used on the wrists was distinctive, a gaudy affair
featuring the emblems of three Canadian provinces. It is hard

to imagine anyone wearing it without somebody remembering having seen it.

The head wrapping consisted of two fringed green cloths each seventy inches long and forty-eight inches in width. When these had been removed, they were found to have been keeping a bloodstained hand towel in place over the lower part of the face; a loose scrap of red-and-white patterned cloth adhered to the hand towel.

The neck was encircled tightly by a decorative linen kitchen towel knotted at the back to form a ligature. Also around the neck, partially under the linen towel but not so tight, ran a loop of flat black plastic-covered wire that had a slight splattering of gray paint. Unknotted, the linen towel was seen to have some kind of ornamental lettering hard to decipher, but eventually identified as Irish Gaelic, spelling out a traditional Irish toast.

Chief Pathologist, Dr. J. Hillsdon Smith, performed the autopsy in Toronto, and his report tells at least something about the dead woman. From an examination of the pelvic bone, her age was established as being between twenty-six and thirty. She had not had a child. Her appendix had been removed. A lively person once, judging from the reddish-blond color she had recently dyed her shoulder-length brown hair, and the remnants of bright pink enamel still clinging to her finger and toe nails. She would have stood a little over five foot three and weighed about a hundred pounds.

By no means a classic beauty, the sketch drawn by a police artist to recreate her looks shows a heavy, broad-jawed face, a pug nose and a short, thick neck. If the artist is correct, she looked several years older than her age. But the forehead is high, the eyes well spaced and the mouth generous.

The forensic dental specialist's report shows that she wore partial dentures in her upper and lower jaw, and that many of her natural teeth had required fillings. As a dentist, the specialist deplored the workmanship of the dentures; as a forensic scientist, he probably welcomed evidence that might make it easier to identify their wearer.

Dr. Hillsdon Smith had found that the woman had died from strangulation. The period during which her body had been in the river was harder to determine. It bore the appearance of a body submersed for one to four weeks, which would mean between April 5 and April 26. If, however, the body had entered the water shortly before the river froze, it might have been there in frozen preservation since late autumn of the previous year.

This, however, seemed unlikely since thirty blood spots on the roadway over the bridge and a splatter of blood on the rail had been found. Assuming these to have come from the victim, the crime must have been committed at some time later than April 19, the last day on which the rainfall had been heavy enough to insure obliteration of the supposed evidence. Unfortunately, the greater certainty that might have been provided by a comparison of blood types was impossible. Blood tests could not be made on the body after its prolonged immersion, nor on the spots on the bridge.

This nevertheless seemed a reasonable assumption which the coroner, Dr. Genier, imaginatively took several degrees further. The assault, he suggested, began by the killer striking the woman in the face with sufficient force to cause a violent nosebleed. The strangling cloth, he went on, had then been knotted tightly enough to produce unconsciousness and eventual death, but not enough to bring the circulatory system to an immediate halt.

Had it done so, the blood would have started to clot; the evidence indicated that the nosebleeding continued heavily enough to make it necessary for the killer to swathe her head in the two large green cloths that might have been normally used as bedspreads. The length of flat plastic-covered wire— by then identified as the type of coaxial cable used by television cable companies for domestic installations—probably represented an ineffective panicked attempt to complete the botched murder.

If these assumptions were correct, the blood on the bridge indicated that the victim was still not quite dead although probably unconscious by the time she had been conveyed to the bridge. But since she could not have survived for more than a very brief time in that precarious state, the coroner's conclusion was that the attack had taken place at a location not far from the bridge.

A seeming objection to this theory is that death had been certified as having been caused by strangulation and not by drowning, but the objection is not necessarily valid. In his classic textbook, *Forensic Medicine,* Dr. Keith Simpson describes several cases in which death "within a few seconds" has occurred in even healthy young persons undergoing unexpected immersion because of a sudden vagal inhibitory mechanism; likelier still to a woman at the point of death. Or the water may have contracted the cloth rapidly enough to strangle her before any quantity of water had entered her lungs. Informed of the coroner's theory, Dr. Hillsdon Smith himself confirmed that it was not inconsistent with his postmortem findings.

By then it seemed that with this ingenious reconstruction, and with the abundance of tangible clues—the "Irish Toast" tea cloth, the flamboyantly emblemed necktie, the paint-splattered coaxial cable, the poor quality dentures and the availability of the woman's fingerprints—it was natural to suppose that not only her identity but that of her clumsy, brutal killer would soon be learned.

Extraordinarily enough, the dead woman's description resembled nobody on the list of missing persons in Canada. Her fingerprints matched none on file. Later the search was extended to the United States. The FBI recognized neither her description nor her prints. A surface patrol of a considerable stretch of the Nation River and an underwater search by six scuba divers failed to find a purse or any personal items her killer may have had to dispose of.

The "Irish Toast" towel and the emblemed necktie were almost equal disappointments. The towel had been manufactured in Ireland, exported to Toronto and distributed to stores in Ottawa, Montreal and Toronto, and nobody had any particular recollection of any specific purchasers. They were cheap items selling at $1.39, and had been stocked for some time. The necktie had been manufactured in Montreal and had been sold by various stores in the province of Quebec and in the eastern part of Ontario. A sales clerk in a store in Marmora did have a memory of selling such a tie to a couple once, and the woman did fit the general description of the unidentified woman. Her companion, it was thought, had been not much taller than her; possibly five foot four or six, and around thirty-five years old. But the sales clerk could not fit a date to the sale. It was all too vague to be considered reliable evidence, but the information was put on record.

No dentist or dental laboratory in the region could be sure of anything about the dentures except that they would not have provided such inferior workmanship themselves. It was frequently remarked that they had probably been produced by an imperfectly qualified technician whose experience had been acquired in the Caribbean or in some other jurisdiction permitting lower standards. A photograph of them was given in dental journals across Canada and later in the United States. All to no avail.

A building-to-building inspection of cable TV installations where similar connecting cable had been installed had been initiated early in the investigation. Hopes ran high when an apartment building was found that had been decorated in a shade of gray that looked the same as that on the speckled band. But a comparison of samples in the forensic laboratory found they were not the same paint.

In this way the inquiry went on, month to month, then year to year. In May 1978, the annual convention of the Ontario Dental Association, attended not only by dentists in the province but by many from other provinces and from the United States, was held in Toronto. By permission of the organizers, a photograph and description of the mysterious dentures were given to all those present, with a request for their help in identifying their possible origin. Once again, a blank. But there was a peculiar sequel; whether or not it had any significance it is impossible to be sure.

A brief account of the police appeal appeared in the Toronto *Sun*. On May 19, the day after the conference had closed, an envelope was found on the desk of a Toronto police station. In it was a clipping of the news story to which had been taped a printed "In Memoriam" card to the memory of a certain lady, "forever remembered, forever missed by the family," whose first names followed: two male and two female.

It seems inappropriate to give the names since it was found that the notice referred to a lady whose death had not occurred until the year after the unidentified body was taken out of the Nation River, and police inquiries established no connection between the two deaths. In all probability, the clipping and the card had been left by somebody badly disturbed. Bizarre communications of this kind having nothing to do with reality are not unusual. On the other hand, there is a faint possibility of an unrevealed connection.

The episode belongs to the story, however, by providing the only semblance of a new clue that the Criminal Investigation Branch of the Ontario Provincial Police has been offered in their search for the killer of the Casselman floater.

The case is too rich in scene-of-the-crime evidence for it to be abandoned lightly. The emblemed tie and the "Irish Toast" tea towel are the kind of articles likely to have been purchased as souvenirs by a tourist; the professional opinions expressed on the dentures suggest that their wearer was probably a foreigner or foreign-born, or a Canadian who had lived for some years in another country.

She could have been a visitor whose relatives and friends at home, unaware of a decision to visit Canada, have been pursuing their inquiries about her well-being elsewhere. Unlikely, perhaps. But no more so than a disappearance nobody has reported, or a woman nobody remembers seeing.

Whoever the victim was, she was the object of a vicious,

brutal murder, and a decisive break in the case may still come
at any time. Until then—or at any future date it might be decided that the case can be considered closed—it will remain
on the active file, and Body Number 074, the Casselman
floater, may yet provide the evidence necessary to convict the
killer.

A year earlier, another gruesome watery discovery was
made which indirectly led to another disappearance, and to
the laying of two murder charges seven years later. At the
time of writing, one of those warrants has still to be served.
Perhaps it never can be. Whatever the final outcome of that
case, oddly enough, it will leave unsolved a mystery—a riddle
which at one time was not regarded as a mystery at all.

On June 17, 1974, a severed human leg was washed
ashore from Lake Ontario. Clearly, it had belonged to a white
adult male, and examination in the forensic laboratories
showed that the rough amputation had been performed after
death. Its condition indicated that it had only been in the
water for a matter of weeks. Little enough to work on, but
Michael Donnelly, a respected real estate broker in north-
western Toronto, had reported that his thirty-two-year-old
younger brother Robert had been missing from the beginning
of May.

Robert had been the black sheep of a large family. He
was a loan shark and a heavy gambler: probably a frequent
cause of concern to his brother, but his life-style only added
to Michael Donnelly's worries when he unaccountably disappeared from sight. Robert had told Michael of the bad blood
that existed between him and Ronald McGuire, another loan
shark, and McGuire's twenty-seven-year-old sister, Mary
Kathleen Misener, fellow members of a gambling club known
as The Circle. Kathy Misener had in fact openly said she
would like to see Robert Donnelly at the bottom of the lake.
From the outset Michael had been convinced Robert had
been murdered. Now it seemed his suspicion might have been
justified.

The date of Robert Donnelly's disappearance and his

physical appearance both came within the limits estimated in the pathologist's report, and shoes belonging to the missing man were a good fit on the severed limb. After careful examination and measurement, a qualified podiatrist was able to say that the foot in question would have produced exactly the wear-marks he had found in the corresponding shoes. In his experience, these were sufficiently distinctive to provide a positive identification.

From the police viewpoint this did not make Ronald McGuire or Kathleen Misener more than strong suspects in a suspected murder. The medical evidence could prove that the original owner of the leg was dead, and the podiatrist's findings gave reason to believe that owner had been Robert Donnelly. (Although a defense lawyer could probably find another podiatrist to dispute this.) But there was nothing to prove that death was the result of murder, and only circumstantial evidence that even if that were true, either McGuire or his sister might be responsible.

Irreparable harm would result from a premature arrest because accused people are entitled to a speedy trial. If acquitted, as they surely would be in this instance, they would be free from any danger of facing trial again on the same charge, even if proof of outright guilt later became available. The disappearance and suspected murder of Robert Donnelly accordingly remained an open case—not shelved but, for the time being, carefully watched on the back burner in the expectation of further developments. The likely discovery of other parts of the body would make identification more positive, a falling out between McGuire, Misener or any of their known associates might lead to somebody talking, or some different act of lawlessness on the part of any of them could provide the break the police needed.

To Michael Donnelly, convinced to the point of obsession of the guilt of McGuire and his sister, the failure of the police to take decisive action was so galling that he took it upon himself to pursue investigations. His initiative was rewarded. As a result of his shadowing Kathy Misener and her lover one night in the fall of 1974 to a motel on the Kingston Road, the police were told of a meeting he had overheard at which Misener, her lover, McGuire and another man had hatched a cold-blooded plan to burn a $100,000 sailboat and murder a lawyer.

The reason for this freakish proposal only emerged later. It appeared that in 1973 McGuire, in his capacity as a loan shark, had advanced a certain Mr. Trim $20,000 to enable him to complete the building of a catamaran against the security of the boat itself, and Trim had fallen in arrears. The yacht, having turned out to be a singularly handsome vessel, became the object of McGuire's desire, and he seized it. When in due course Trim came up with the cash needed to discharge his loan, McGuire waved the money away, asserting that the sailboat was now his legal property; a $100,000 beauty was acquired for the few thousand dollars remaining to pay off the debt.

Trim sought legal advice and took McGuire to court on a repossession order issued by his lawyer, Victor Paisley. McGuire defended the action, lying outrageously to retain the boat. Paisley exposed him twice as a barefaced perjurer without any difficulty, and on each occasion he had been sent briefly to jail to purge his offense. It was virtually certain that at the next hearing Trim's action would succeed.

Most moneylenders in McGuire's position would have faced this outcome with a shrug of resignation ("You win some, you lose some"), but that was not the McGuire way. McGuire and his sister did not take defeat lightly; defeat was an insult to be avenged. The first part of the solution, as they saw it, was to burn the boat for the insurance money. The second part, which involved a question of honor, had to be a contract for the lawyer, Victor Paisley, to be killed.

Happily, the police had had advance warning because of Michael Donnelly's enterprise, but the neo-Borgian plot would have failed anyway, because one of the co-conspirators had second thoughts about its wisdom. This, coming on the heels of the police inquiries into the fate of Robert Donnelly, probably influenced Ronald McGuire's decision to sail the prized catamaran into southern waters.

In January 1975, he took off on a cruise to the Bahamas. Or so he announced. Where, if anywhere, he subsequently dropped anchor is uncertain. A few days later, Ronald McGuire's name was officially listed among the world's missing persons. He has vanished, it seems, into thin air. A disappearing trick? It may be. There are accommodating South American jurisdictions. But, as we have seen in other instances—remember "Unusual Disturbance in Forest Hill"—citizens engaged in moneylending and professional gambling appear to acquire enemies prepared to go to quite elaborate lengths to settle their differences. All that can be said for sure is that from the day of his departure until this time of writing, nobody knows the whereabouts of Ronald McGuire.

Obviously a principal in the plot to murder Victor Paisley (there were associated villainous diversions, such as a diversionary bombing of an automobile), McGuire's disappearance inevitably slowed the process of the law. To Michael Donnelly's mounting vexation, it was not until March 1981 that the Crown decided to proceed with the case against the other principal, Mary Kathleen Misener, on four charges: conspiracy to commit murder, counseling murder, conspiracy to commit arson and counseling to commit arson. The murder conspiracy charge, of course, referred to the lawyer, Victor Paisley, not Robert Donnelly although his brother, who had overheard the meeting at the motel where the plot had been hatched, was to be a key witness.

Ironically, it was to be Michael Donnelly, who had been so valuable to the Crown in bringing the case to trial, who at this point was almost responsible for scuttling it because of his pent-up indignation.

Asked by the Crown whether he had brothers or sisters, he replied correctly that he had had three sisters and three brothers, but that one of them was dead. Then, before the Crown prosecutor could restrain him, he burst out, "The accused murdered one of my brothers. I now have *two* brothers and three sisters." The judge followed the only possible course by declaring a mistrial and ordering a change of venue.

At the second hearing of the case in London, Ontario, the next month, the jury found Kathleen Misener guilty. The sentence amounted to six years in the penitentiary, five for conspiring to commit murder and the sixth for conspiring to commit arson.

Her conviction on the comparatively minor conspiracy charges put the remarkable case of the missing limb into a quite different perspective. In August 1981, Kathleen Misener, now in penitentiary, was charged with the first-degree murder of Robert Gerrard Donnelly. Even if not entirely unexpected, this must have given her cause for thought.

She did indeed know more about Robert Donnelly's disappearance than she had previously admitted. That admission might reduce any additional sentence she might incur. And the disappearance of her brother Ronald in southern climes provided a defense he would scorn her for not recognizing. She decided to talk, and as a result of what she told them, the police learned where they must dig on a farm in Lindsay, Ontario, for the evidence they needed.

Sure enough, exactly at the spot she had told them, the police found human bones, identifiable by dental records as the remains of Robert Donnelly. But there was something astonishing about Robert Donnelly's mortal remains—the skeleton possessed two complete matching leg bones. The severed leg washed ashore in 1974 had belonged to somebody else. This was the crowning irony of the case. For more than seven years, Kathy Misener had known that she had been rightly suspected of some connection with the disappearance of Robert Donnelly on utterly erroneous evidence.

The rest was the conventional anti-climax of plea bargaining. As an accessory after the fact, Misener pleaded guilty to a realization that her brother had beaten Donnelly to death and buried his body, but denied any knowledge of his intentions before the killing took place. She admitted driving Donnelly's car to New York, and abandoning it in the parking lot at the JFK airport, but claimed to have done so only at her brother's request, and for all the prosecution could prove, that was exactly the way it had been. Thus, as an accessory after the fact to a murder, she drew an additional sentence of four years. Based on the evidence that she had given, a warrant was issued for the arrest of Ronald McGuire on a first-degree murder charge.

Will that warrant ever be served? Staff Inspector James Crawford of Toronto Metro Homicide has recent information indicating McGuire is very much alive, and keeps the warrant handy.

The no less fascinating mystery that is in danger of being overlooked, however, surrounds the severed leg washed ashore from Lake Ontario. For seven years the police believed it was tangible evidence that Robert Donnelly was dead, probably murdered. He had been the only man on the missing persons list in June 1974, whose description matched the pathologist's findings, and its discovery prompted all that followed. But it was not his.

It came from a corpse. Whose?

A Girl We'll Call
Miranda

Like all the disappearances described in this book, this is true. In this case, however, part of the story happened twice; once, in fiction, to a twenty-year-old art student in the cellars of a country cottage in Sussex, England; once, in real life, just as horribly, to a twelve-year-old schoolgirl in a cellar under a garage in a smallish community somewhere in Canada sometime during the 1970s. The actual date could only be of interest as the year in which John Fowles's first novel, *The Collector*, appeared in a paperback edition. Although that, for all we know, may be just a coincidence.

The central figure in the novel was a shy and painfully inhibited young municipal clerk whose only observable pleasure, until he won a fortune on the football pools, was butterfly collecting. Some he bred, some he caught; sooner or later, he always killed them, mounted them with delicate care and photographed them. His secret pleasure was to fantasize a life with the exquisite girl with long, pale, silky hair who lived in the townhouse across the road from the council offices where he performed the routine duties of his junior position.

The life he consciously fantasized was astonishingly placid and genteel. An only child, he had been raised by a mean-spirited and censorious aunt to understand that sex was a dirty, vulgar procedure repulsive to self-respecting people;

part of his pale-haired idol's attraction was that as a member of the upper class she could be expected to share this view. Whenever he caught his unconscious fantasies straying beyond the bounds of decorum, he hastily repressed the image.

His huge winnings suddenly seemed to make it possible for everything to come true. He bought an isolated cottage and equipped its underground cellars with tasteless luxuries. Securely sealed off from the outside world, he transformed it into a gigantic specimen cage in which a collector could spend all day if he chose, enjoying the grace and gossamer beauty of the most perfect specimen ever captured.

The girl, cunningly trapped by the experienced collector, steeled herself for the commonplace rape and violence she supposed in store, but gradually realized the strange truth. She had become the adored captive of a creature of such limited vision that he had never given a thought to how the venture should be ended; in his mind it ran forever. He was sly enough to intercept her pleas for help, shallow-minded enough to withstand her efforts to rouse some human response through art, music, literature or religion, and both prudish and incontinent enough to be only deeply shocked by her attempt to seduce him.

He had failed, though, to be careful enough in protecting her health. Within three months, she had died from pneumonia (he could not call a doctor), and was buried deep in the large garden under the apple trees. He was upset about it all for a little while until he saw that it wasn't really his fault. As the book closes, he is toying with the idea that the shopgirl he has seen in Woolworth's might prove to be a more satisfactory houseguest next time. . . .

In *The Collector*, the girl's name was Miranda, and the collector himself was Frederick. So in this account of what happened in Canada, the twelve-year-old schoolgirl will also be called Miranda, and, for her sake only, her captor will be called Frederick, although he was forty-three—fifteen years older than his fictional counterpart.

Frederick won no large sum of money, but he had no

need of a fortune to make his fantasies a reality. At the height of the Cold War, he had, like thousands of others, fashioned a concrete-lined air-raid shelter below the garage attached to his house. Nothing elaborate; barely six feet high, and offering little more space than required to contain a six-foot bunk, a small table and chair, a sink, a chemical toilet beneath a wall cupboard and a rickety ladder tall enough to reach the ceiling trap. Of course, unventilated, and the only illumination a bare 60-watt light bulb. Moisture oozed around a threadbare piece of carpeting.

Frederick shared the house itself with his wife and her three children by an earlier marriage. His wife was aware of the hours Frederick often spent building campers in the garage since this was his livelihood. She had also once had knowledge of the underground cellar, but apparently thought it had been sealed up. It would have made little difference; its three hundred or so cubic feet of space offered little prospect of survival for a household of five in the event of hostilities of any duration.

It was long before Miranda's disappearance that Frederick had been struck by the fancy of how well the space below his garage floor could serve as a stage for some of his bizarre fantasies, he was to say later. Not exactly in those words, of course. ("I had been thinking for some time of using it to confine a girl," he later admitted.)

Accordingly, he had moved his workbench over the trapdoor to the cellar so that the shelving of a paint locker stood over the trap. He made the shelving removable, but indistinguishable from the shelving along the rest of the lockers. He had fixed bolts on the outside of the trapdoor, so that it could not be lifted from below, and lined the inside of the trap with two inches of fabric-covered foam insulation to make it soundproof. The rest of the ceiling was concrete.

It is interesting at this point to see how the fictional Frederick in *The Collector* dealt with a corresponding problem. His specimen was to be housed in an inner cellar, so he fitted a two-inch-thick oak door with a sheet metal lining on the inside and ten-inch bolts outside. Then, chuckling at his ingenuity, he constructed a dummy bookcase on the outside to make the doorway seem like a cabinet in a wall recess. The lightweight wooden structure was designed to be quickly removable. Obvious enough precautions for either man to take, perhaps, but the similarity of methods is striking.

In real life the preparations unfortunately were taken several stages further. Brackets were firmly mounted on the cement wall, one on either side at the head of the bed. Another bracket was mounted on the wall halfway down the length of the bed. Slender chains were fixed to each of the brackets, and other furnishings included a dog collar, two sets of handcuffs and eight belts.

In the novel, the collector knew who was going to occupy the cellar long before he started to make it ready for her arrival. There is no way of being sure whether this was so in real life, but probability lies in that direction. Little Miranda, a quiet, serious girl in the seventh grade of the local elementary school, was the youngest of the three daughters of a family living on the same block as Frederick, and he could have noticed her any day on her way to and from school, just as the fictional Frederick watched his adored specimen leaving and entering the house across the road from his office window.

The schoolgirl, too shy and cautious to hitchhike or accept the offer of a lift from a stranger, similarly knew Frederick well enough to return a friendly greeting. She could not have known that he had received psychiatric treatment in the past, or that the local police had been called to his home in the early hours of the morning some eighteen months previously when he had been threatening to shoot his wife and her three children. She was probably aware that Frederick's wife and her own mother were on friendly visiting terms, and that might have seemed reason enough to accept Frederick's good-natured offer to drive her to school that chilly day.

School absences seldom concern anybody but parents and the school authorities; often they are frequent enough to arouse more irritation than alarm. With Miranda, it was different. It was known that she had left home in good time, had no reason and had shown no inclination to skip her classes; nevertheless, nobody had seen her on the road. Within hours, police were on the lookout, and over the next few days the total of policemen and volunteers taking part in the search exceeded a hundred.

Eventually the local police chief, certain that the explanation of the girl's disappearance lay close to her home (why else had nobody seen her at an hour when the streets had been far from empty?) but had been missed, ordered an entirely new team to restart the inquiry from scratch.

As the nearest neighbor with a record of erratic behavior, Frederick had already been closely questioned. But Frederick was a cool one. Standing at his garage workbench only feet above his imprisoned captive, he answered the policeman's questions thoughtfully and with an air of concerned helpfulness. When a second policeman took him over his previous statement and asked further questions, his performance was equally smooth.

Too smooth, it seems some felt. Certainly so smooth as to make it impossible to discern cracks that might give a clue where a break in the case might be found. The investigation proceeded with Frederick's name always on the list of suspects. But suspicion of what crime? Almost inevitably, with no demand for ransom, no reason to run away from home and no reported accident, the grim assumption would have to be murder.

Nothing in Canadian criminal history would have prompted a suspicion of the charges Frederick would finally face. A murder with no eyewitnesses and no tangible evidence demands a strategy of its own of which the main components are sometimes watchfulness and psychological pressure. Time is on the side of police in such cases. Tragically, this was not one of those cases.

Frederick was no fastidious collector like his fictional counterpart. The brackets, chains, handcuffs and straps indicate clearly enough that his aims were not centered on preserving the beauty and the pristine sheen of his specimen or, like the butterfly collector, photographing her in exciting poses. Nor, indeed, had he set his mind on a fully grown adult of the species. He had gone for what he knew he could handle, what he thought he could discipline, what he may even have hoped to impress.

Like a boy with a new pet, Frederick visited Miranda frequently at first, bringing her a radio, chocolate bars and a copy of *Reader's Digest*. Food was always a problem, but there was hot water from the sink and there were always instant soup mixes. Soup made from hot tap water, in fact, provided the only hot meals Miranda was to have for the next six months.

In the novel, the butterfly collector tries to satisfy the original Miranda by promising her a specific date on which he will release her. In real life, Frederick told his captive that he was holding her for ransom "to get enough money to buy his wife a camper," and that she would be released as soon as the money was paid. Later, to assure her how much she was missed, he gave her a copy of the "Missing" notice offering $8,500 reward for information leading to her discovery.

The parallels between fiction and fact go further, almost as if the twelve-year-old schoolgirl had known how the twenty-year-old art student behaved in captivity. "Do you believe in God?" the woman had asked, and the Collector had shrugged and answered, "Not much." Persisting, she had said, "It must be yes or no." And with infuriating stupidity, the Collector could only say, "I don't think about it. Don't see that it matters."

As it happened, the real life Miranda was of a strongly religious nature, a member, like her sisters, of a fundamentalist congregation. She persisted with her captor more earnestly than the fictional art student. No amount of sneering weakened her belief and when her unsophisticated arguments were derided, she tried to continue the debate on paper, writing on a flower-decorated sheet of pink notepaper from the satchel she had been carrying when she had set out for school.

Addressing the letter to him by his first name, she wrote:

> I know you think I'm stupid and, like you say, everybody is entitled to their own thoughts. But I do believe in God and I believe in friends. I just wish you would be my friend. I also know that I will get out of here and so I'm not worried. God has helped me so far and will help me to finish. God works in mysterious ways but what he does is right.
>
> P.S. I know that you don't believe in God but I'll just say that God will be with you.

The letter was contained in a matching pink envelope on which she had written: "Happy days are always here." An amazing child. One that senses that in selecting his victim, the wispy, balding real-life Frederick had as badly mismatched himself in spirit as did the fictional collector, and suspects that his fantasies never attained the liveliness that he had once imagined.

Frederick was under outside pressures as well. Policemen continued to question and requestion him. Once in the course of a search, the door of the paint locker was opened and the interior scrutinized. But the officer, having already checked that the shelves of the other lockers under the workbench were stationary, did not think to lift the heavy cans that were all that held down the removable shelf.

Perhaps that was the worst of many tense moments at the start. Certainly it was close to the time Frederick was admitted to hospital for an overdose of sleeping pills. He had soon recovered, but for those few days Miranda was wondering if she would ever see daylight, or her family or even food ever again. After his discharge from hospital care, the visits began again, but now he was drinking more heavily. Often, when he climbed down the ladder unsteadily, it was with a bottle of vodka in one hand.

There were days, sometimes several days at a stretch now, when he did not visit her at all. Sometimes he would have left a packet of instant soup mix or some chocolate bars, sometimes not. Month after month . . . another back issue of *Reader's Digest* would be added to a growing pile.

In total, Miranda probably had to spend close to four thousand hours in solitude during her captivity in that small underground room, sometimes unventilated for days. It would have been easy to lose all count of time, but she made a small ballpoint mark on the palm of one hand to count the days. (The final count showed that she was only four days out over the entire period.) Nevertheless, reality became hazy. Once Frederick, his wife and the family went off for a vacation. It was Miranda's impression that she had been left alone for six weeks, but subsequent evidence from neighbors indicated that the period may have been only a fortnight.

Prayer almost certainly occupied some of those hours, but even for such an unusual child, there could not be enough prayers to span so vast a void. There were the *Reader's Digests.* On a shelf was a book titled, *You Can Change Your Life Through Psychic Power.* Occasionally there was a newspaper. But best of all there was the radio and the twenty-four-hour-a-day rock programs from a nearby station. Miranda learned the words of every song that attained popularity over those six months.

How did Frederick pass the time? He seems to have been taking a perverse pleasure from making sure that Miranda's disappearance continued to occupy the minds of the neighborhood. Every school morning he was out in his car offering the children lifts to school. "Can't have any more of you vanishing!" he would cry. Miranda's two sisters were frequently invited.

All the families on the block kept up their friendships. Miranda's sisters continued to go out with Frederick's step-daughters, Miranda's mother continued to visit Frederick's wife, and they would sip tea together, both unaware that Miranda was confined in dirt and squalor a few feet away.

Frederick himself was also drinking even more heavily by then. He was still on probation as a result of the charge brought against him for threatening his wife and step-children with a revolver. Now she was frequently calling his probation officer to complain of his aggressive behavior, and asking for his arrest.

It is unlikely that when he was readying his dungeon for his captive, the real-life Frederick had any more idea than his fictional predecessor how the enacted fantasy could be concluded without risk to himself. In reading the history of events, however, it is hard to avoid the ugly suspicion that, consciously or unconsciously, the final curtain was taking shape in his mind in at least the second half of Miranda's captivity.

She was not providing the exciting pleasures he had expected. Spouting that nonsense about Jesus and wanting to be his friend. It is not surprising that he was visiting her less often and even then, what with that horrid smell and everything, more to see that she had something to eat than anything else.

"Not in my nature to kill anyone; can't even bear to see anybody die," he may have reassured himself. "But you have to wonder, anyone as sick and weak as this one's getting, whether they wouldn't really be better off dead. She can't go long without food, not in the state she's reached. Nobody knows she's down there. Supposing that for some reason, not my fault, I just couldn't give her any soup or chocolate for a long time, it would just be she died a natural death, and I couldn't really blame myself for it. Once I made sure I couldn't help her anymore, I could just leave her there. After a bit, I could seal the old trap up and cement it over, and after a time there wouldn't even be any more smell."

Subconscious thought along those lines might possibly have started as far back as the time when he spent a few days in hospital after the overdose of sleeping pills. According to his neighbors, he was only away with his family on vacation for two weeks; according to Miranda, she went without food for six weeks at that time. Was she really wholly mistaken? Is it possible that his behavior in the last few weeks before his arrest was half intended to provoke his probation officer into having him arrested and sent to prison for breaching the terms of his parole? In Miranda's condition at the end, it seems unlikely that her faith would have sustained her without nutrition for many more days.

On the one hundred and eightieth day of Miranda's captivity, Frederick climbed down the ladder for the first time for several days and left her a chocolate bar. By now she was extremely weak, and only able to crawl from the bed.

The next day Frederick started drinking early and continued through the day. By evening, he had become the loud, aggressive brawler his wife knew would soon turn into the self-pitying whiner. About ten o'clock he declared his intention of killing himself with the loaded gun he kept in the garage. He left the house, and silence ensued.

As so often before, she dialed the police station and within minutes two members of the tactical squad were around. Finding the garage door locked, they kicked it open, but saw the work space was empty. After a cursory look around, they concluded it was another false alarm, left and made their way back to their car.

Frederick's wife heard them start to drive away in disbelief. She had heard Frederick enter the garage, and knew he must be there. She left the house, entered the garage and this time saw the open locker cabinet, with its base removed and the trapdoor wide. Peering down, she saw Frederick's feet splayed horizontally, and concluded he had done precisely what he had threatened. She hurried back into the house and called the police station again to explain what she had seen.

The radio call caught the squad car before it was far away from the house; with a squeal of brakes, the car reversed its direction. The two policemen reentered the garage just at the moment when Frederick's drawn and bemused face was emerging from the open trapdoor. He was seized at once for questioning, but before he had time to speak, both officers heard a pitiful mewling sound like that of a wounded animal coming from the darkness from which Frederick had emerged. Slowly, painfully, a little figure clothed in a sweater and green slacks climbed up the ladder and blinked around, as if half-blind.

"My God, Bill," said one policeman to the other, "it's Miranda." He was the officer who had taken the original "Missing Person" report.

With their attention momentarily distracted, Frederick made a dash for a side wall, reaching for an upper shelf. The two policemen seized him before his arms were fully extended, in time to prevent him from grabbing the loaded rifle stored there in readiness.

Miranda saw her home and family again sometime before midnight, and the next day was taken to stay with relatives in another town. She was too weak to do more than crawl and unable to raise her voice above a whisper. It would be a long time before her physical health returned. She was now thirteen, but she would probably never have the outlook of other children the same age.

The day after his arrest Frederick was transferred to a regional correction center to await trial on charges of kidnapping, abduction, rape, gross indecency and unlawfully taking away a female person against her will with intent to have illicit sexual relations with her. Four days later he was found in his cell bleeding copiously from a deep slash on his inner arm near the elbow and transferred to hospital. The next day he was reported to be in fair condition.

His trial came four months later. Some plea bargaining had taken place since all those concerned both with the prosecution and the defense wanted the girl to be spared the ordeal of examination and cross-examination. On his counsel's advice, Frederick pleaded guilty to charges reduced to kidnapping and having sexual intercourse with a girl under fourteen. It made no real difference to the outcome, since he received the maximum penalty of life imprisonment with the judge's recommendation that he should be transferred to the appropriate psychiatric center.

During the course of the trial, the court listened to a note that Miranda had written. If she survived her ordeal, she said, she intended to donate her life to Christ.

At no time in the previous year did Frederick seem closer to the fictional butterfly collector than in the final statement he provided for the prosecution. "I wanted to make her happy by keeping her from the world," he said. And, as one who wished to be totally fair, he added, "I don't think I did her any good, mind you, but I don't think it did any harm."

His appeal of the life sentence was unanimously rejected with the chief justice telling his defense counsel that his client should never be released from prison. It was then revealed that Frederick had a history of sexual offenses going back to his early twenties.

The whole case poses dark riddles. Do the sleeping-pill overdose and the arm-slashing suggest that Frederick could feel remorse and shame like other men? More probably perhaps, they were instinctive responses to an urge to escape blame, retribution and the treatment he might expect from fellow prisoners. If Frederick entertained the idea of deliberately allowing Miranda to die from neglect and starvation—and that can only be speculation—why was the course not pursued more actively? The answer might be that he wanted death to be "by accident." It is possible to suppose his irrational behavior in the final days was the consequence of despair and an urge to be discovered. Perhaps he had found himself incapable of the final, resolute actions to end Miranda's life. Why else leave the trapdoor open for his wife to see him recumbent below on his final descent into Miranda's dungeon?

All riddles with no sure answers. They also raise a further puzzling question: If the trap was thrown back as the wife described, how could it be possible that the two policemen did not immediately see it when they first broke down the garage door?

Roundup

A popular myth, encouraged by a great deal of crime fiction and television, says that a missing-person report cannot be officially entered until a rigidly fixed number of hours has elapsed since the person was last seen or expected to arrive. This is not so. The closer in age the person is to either of the extremes of life, or the clearer the possibility of a crime or serious accident, the greater is the promptness and intensity of the search.

The investigation of disappearances is, of course, only one of many routine daily functions the police handle in addition to the investigation of crimes, traffic accidents and sudden deaths. (The daunting list extends from traffic control and driving offenses, escort services to prisons and mental hospitals, and court security to the unloved tasks of summons serving, court testimony and report writing.) Nevertheless, every reported disappearance coming within the powers of the police to investigate must be taken seriously from the outset because of its potential to develop into a matter of graver concern.

While it is true there will be those who express alarm too frequently and too soon, senior policemen will tell you that they are to be preferred to those who delay too long. Like firemen, the police accept false alarms as a necessary part of the job. When the danger proves real, the speed of their response may be the only hope of averting or minimizing it. Where injuries have been sustained in an accident in some remote, seldom traveled area, for instance, hopes for recovery can depend greatly on how soon treatment can be provided. If the child or adult has been the victim of criminal violence, a life may be saved.

Even if it proves too late to prevent a tragedy, the likelihood of apprehending the attacker is greatly increased if the investigation is started while evidence is undisturbed and memories are fresh. In the big majority of cases researched for this book, the unpleasant possibility of grave danger appeared to have been fully recognized. This seems to be reflected in the high overall recovery rate on missing-person statistics, although these successes seldom receive much publicity. For the most part, an efficiently and happily solved disappearance is a non-news item. Undeniably, there have also been failures, which inevitably attract greater attention.

In some of these, it can be seen in hindsight that errors of judgment occurred and leads were overlooked. In others, the investigation was badly impaired because of a delay in notification. But it also becomes apparent that the investigation of a disappearance can be among the most puzzling tasks that the police are required to undertake when it proves to be something that has not been solved by common sense and footwork within the first few hours.

In the initial stages, it is seldom possible to be sure whether the disappearance is voluntary or the consequence of accident or criminal violence. If evidence of the latter is found and the victim is a child, the probability—but only the probability—will be that the attacker was a stranger, possibly someone who had never been seen with the child before. The attacker rarely proves to have derived any tangible benefit from causing the disappearance. It is not known where the disappearance took place; if interviews produce evidence, it is often unreliable or contradictory.

A further point. Lakes, marshes, forests and remote areas all offer places of concealment for a body that may lie hidden if not forever then for long enough to delay discovery and destroy the evidence of violence. Something that became disturbingly evident in the course of researching this material is that a body does not have to be particularly deeply buried to remain undetected by police dogs, air survey or other means of site identification, even when the search has been confined to a comparatively narrow area.

Although not recently, some local police authorities have invited clairvoyants and psychics to see if they can succeed where routine methods have failed, usually in response to public feeling and a parent's emotional distress. There are indeed accounts of such intervention producing inexplicably accurate information, but it has to be said that no record of any such event in recent Canadian criminal investigation was encountered, although there is mention of several failures.

One of the possibilities often heard suggested to explain a prolonged disappearance is that the missing person is suffering from amnesia. It is true that some disappearances—although possibly fewer than have been claimed—have been caused by amnesia, usually induced by shock, emotional tension, a brain injury or illness. However, unless the sufferer has the misfortune of being in a remote region, amnesiacs are seldom missing for long. They are always distressingly aware of their mental blackout, and the mounting confusion that ensues either drives them to seek help or engage in behavior that advertises their need of it.

One summer's evening in the 1970s, the young son of a small storeowner saw his fourteen-year-old sister talking to a local youth they both knew, a nineteen-year-old truck driver. He saw the girl enter the truck which drove away, and he told his parents about it when his sister failed to return that evening. The father reported the girl's absence to the police.

Questioned the next day, the youth said the girl had asked him to drive her to a beach about twenty miles away, where he had left her. A widespread search of the beach and the surrounding area produced no sign of the girl or evidence from anybody who might have seen her.

Just seven days later, she was found wandering round an arts-and-crafts exhibition more than two hundred miles away. She was in good physical shape apart from some bruises on her neck, but appeared to be dazed and unable to give her name or say where she lived. Neither, apparently, did she know where she was then, nor how she came to be there. The local police were quickly able to identify her from the recently circulated "missing" notice, and within a few hours she was on her way home.

What had occurred since she had been away is uncertain. Further official inquiries were made unnecessary by the fact that four days earlier—the day after he had been questioned by the police—the young truck driver had blown his head off with a shotgun.

The symptoms and treatment of amnesia are familiar to medical science, but the lightning recovery of memory encountered in fiction is never experienced in real life. Recovery is at best gradual.

Rarer and more baffling are the handful of cases, investigated and described by experienced psychiatrists, of freak memory failures which have allowed individuals to take on new identities quite naturally and unaware of their previous lives—and subsequently revert to their original identities without realizing anything unusual has interrupted their daily routine.

The condition is known as a fugue (or flight), classified by psychiatrists as a dissociative form of hysterical neurosis. It is often accompanied by a striking change in personality. In rare cases the victim of the fugue takes on not one, but two, three or even more separate identities in a bewildering sequence; these, of course, are the famous multiple-personality phenomena that have provided the basis for films and novels. None seem to have involved a reported disappearance, but one instance of a dual-personality fugue, occurring in the last

century, definitely did. It was investigated and described by
the famous psychiatrist William James, brother of the novelist
Henry James. Although it did not occur in Canada, it is
sufficiently unusual to be related.

The Reverend Ansel Bourne was a much respected evangelist in Providence, Rhode Island, where he had lived blame-
lessly for a quarter of a century. One day in 1887 he suddenly
disappeared.

A considerable time later one of his flock, who happened
to be in a small town a few hundred miles away in Pennsyl-
vania, entered a stationer's shop to make a purchase, and was
astonished to see that the shopkeeper politely attending to his
needs was the evangelist. Greeted by name, however, the
shopkeeper seemed genuinely puzzled and assured the cus-
tomer that he was mistaken. The name of Ansel Bourne was
quite unfamiliar to him.

Months later, the Reverend Ansel Bourne reappeared in
Providence, calmly setting about his regular affairs as if he
had never been away; indeed, it proved that he had no recollection of where he had been or of anything that he had done
in the intervening period.

When the strange interlude was investigated, it was
found that the evangelist had quietly appeared in the town
where nobody had previously known him and proceeded to
rent retail premises, and then to stock them with a full range
of stationery, all with the appearance of a man fully acquainted with his trade. His arrival had aroused no particular
interest. He handled his business with seeming competence
and behaved generally as a good but unassertive citizen.

Interestingly, it was learned that during his absence, he
had become a member of the Religious Society of Friends,
more generally known as Quakers. He attended regularly, but
was remembered more as an attentive and respectful listener
than as a leader of discussion. The Religious Society of
Friends claims that no theologically trained priest or outward
religious rites are needed to establish communion between
the soul and its God. Perhaps this throws some light on the

cause of the Reverend Ansel Bourne's fugue. But the rest remains a mystery.

It is a story which at face value invites suspicion; by popular legend, the credulity of psychiatrists and the morality of the clergy are both notoriously open to temptation. No doubt whispers to this effect circulated at the time. But the manner of the clergyman's life during the period of fugue seems to have been a model of decorum, and his reputation before and after his disappearance appears to be unblemished, so a motive is hard to perceive. And it may be safely assumed that William James approached the case with his usual scientific skepticism: with such unusual material he would have taken particular care to protect his well-established reputation against any charge of inadequate investigation. His conclusions, moreover, match those of other investigators of fugue episodes.

Short of dismissing a considerable body of scientific evidence, therefore, the possibility exists of the "victim" of a disappearance to be unaware of having been reported as a missing person under a different identity and to be living contentedly elsewhere. Since the days of Ansel Bourne, however, distances have narrowed and means of communication increased so greatly that it is unlikely for a fugue to continue unrecognized for so long today.

Nevertheless, it is clear that when someone is missing, nobody can be absolutely sure of the explanation. The disappearance may have been voluntary or involuntary. Even if the latter, harm has not necessarily been sustained either by accident or malice. Cases involving violence are those holding the elements of drama and have supplied most of the material for this collection. Once more, however, it must be emphasized that these are the exceptions. The vast majority of disappearances are temporary, almost all are relatively brief and most have happy endings.

On the other hand, it is as well to remember that of the 240 people likely to be reported missing in Canada, probably six or seven will be unlucky enough to provide the exceptions. Do at least try not to be among them.